Florida Writers Association

Writing Our History

One Writer at a Time

Second Ten Years, 2011 to 2021

FWA | FLORIDA WRITERS ASSOCIATION

Writing Our History

One Writer at a Time

Second Ten Years, 2011–2021

Florida Writers Association

Graphic design and publication format by Arielle Haughee.
Interior Formatting by Autumn Skye.
Compilation coordinated by John Hazen.

For information regarding permission contact us at our website:
www.FloridaWritersAssociation.org, or write to:
Florida Writers Association
Attention Publisher
PO Box 66069
St. Pete Beach, FL 33736-6069

ISBN: 978-1-7375305-2-7
Library of Congress Control Number: 2021945631
Printed in the USA
Printed September 2021

Acknowledgments

by *John Hazen*
Book Compilation Coordinator

Special recognition is extended to Chrissy Jackson, FWA Past President and current Vice President of Finance, for her vision and dedication throughout the development and production of this volume. John Hazen and Su Gerheim provided significant contributions in the writing and editing process. Paul Iasevoli, Mark Newhouse, Michael Farrell and Linda Feist all contributed personal stories about how FWA has affected them. Mary Ann de Stefano provided past copies of the Florida Writer. Arielle Haughee provided valuable assistance in the formatting, graphics and cover design. Chris Coward created the text on the Royal Palm Literary Awards. Tami Lowe provided copy for the Book Silent Auction.

Appreciation is extended to the Group Leaders and writers group members who provided photos and contributions.

Table of Contents

Section One

Introduction, Personal Impact of FWA

Introduction

by Rick Bettencourt
President, Florida Writers Association

Welcome to the Florida Writer Association's twentieth year!

I think you'll find this book a fun way to celebrate our two decades together. For any organization to grow like we have is a huge accomplishment, and for it to be done by an all-volunteer organization is amazing.

In 2013, I discovered FWA. I had recently transplanted from Massachusetts and was looking for strong writers to workshop a novel I was writing. That summer, I discovered Dona Lee's Manatee County writers group. I found the group fun, engaging, and filled with caring individuals who loved writing and listening to my work.

I joined FWA right away and gravitated to the various webinars given, soaking up a ton of information. When host Jade Kerrion said she needed assistance running them, I rose my hand. In the early days, I worked in the background, monitoring the chat, while she introduced and spoke with speakers. When she decided to step down from leading that area, I took over.

After managing FWA's webinars for a year, former president Cheyenne Knopf Williams tapped me on the shoulder to join the board of directors. Having had board experience with my homeowner's association, I thought it would be a perfect fit. The board learned I was the former treasurer for my HOA, and I was handed FWA's finances.

I served as Vice President of Finance from 2018 to 2020. During that time, we shored up resources for the long-term—including healthy reserves and setting aside funds for key infrastructure, such as our website.

In 2019, we started the process of solutioning for the replacement of our website. We knew strong, automated processes were critical to our growth; and the homegrown systems we had in place were in desperate need of repair.

In the first quarter of 2020, we launched plans with MemberClicks to create a membership system and website that would help us grow into the future. In the spring, I took over the presidency from interim president Larry Kokko to manage the organization through this critical phase.

While 2020 brought us many challenges with Covid-19 and the need to pivot our conference as remote, we kept on track with the system and even delivered early functionality to house the 2020 remote conference.

In January 2021, we launched floridawriters.org with all its bells and whistles.

We look forward to another twenty years being your writing resource.

The Personal Impact of FWA

Much of what the FWA offers writers is professional in nature by helping its members improve their craft. However, FWA touches many members personally as well. Here are a couple examples of where that happened.

Paul's Story

by Paul Iasevoli
Director, 2021 RPLA Rubrics
Coordinator, RPLA Judge Liaison

In May of 2016 my spouse of 34 years died of a sudden heart attack. At the time I was working on a novel. The night before my spouse died, he suggested I quit my job and dedicate myself to my dream of writing. Fast forward six months later when I decided to downsize and sell my house. The real estate agent I chose just happened to know Rick Bettencourt. When she found out I was an aspiring writer, she suggested I meet with him. Rick and I went out for drinks, and he invited me to my first Bradenton Writers Group meeting.

My first visit to the group, I read an excerpt from the novel I was working on, and the group enthusiastically encouraged me to pursue that story. Still in a state of mourning, I decided to work on several chapters of the novel as stand-alone stories and submit them to the 2017 FWA collection and the Royal Palm Literary Awards (RPLA). That year, one was accepted into the Collection and the other won 2nd Place (Silver) for short story in the 2017 RPLA. Needless to say, I was over the moon to have won an award for my writing. I had published several poems in college, but I never thought I could make it as a prose writer.

With the feedback from the RPLA, I reworked the short story that had won 2nd Place and submitted it—on a whim—to Deep South Magazine into their 2018 Race in Place contest and, out of the blue, it won Honorable Mention (3rd Place) from a field of hundreds of entries into their contest. That small accomplishment gave me the courage to pursue publication of my LGBTQ+ novella *Winter Blossoms* with Beaten Track Publishing in 2018. In 2019 *Winter Blossoms* was nominated for Goodreads' best M/M romance—it didn't win, but the recognition was flattering.

In the ensuing years, I've gone on to publish my work in High Shelf Press, Cathexis, City River, Tree, and other literary journals. But no matter what my writing resume may say, I owe all my success to the FWA and fine people like its president Rick Bettencourt and the members of the Bradenton Writers group—especially its leader David Pearce and its former leader Dona Gould-Musitano.

As the Florida Writers Association moves into its third decade, I hope the organization will inspire other writers as it has inspired me.

Linda's Story

by Linda Feist
River City Writers Group Leader

My family and I relocated to Jacksonville, FL in 2007, from the snowy north just outside of Buffalo, NY.

I needed to get serious with my writing, and luckily found the FWA. At this point, I had had a series of essays published in the Buffalo News, but my true love, fiction, was still hibernating in notebooks, computer files, and on scraps of paper.

I thought, what the heck, and entered the short fiction category in the RPLA competition. I became a finalist and attended the writer's conference and banquet.

I didn't get to walk the "red carpet", but the experience encouraged me to go forward with gusto! I reached finalist status five consecutive years, but my "Always a bridesmaid, never a bride," status remained.

Despite not winning a medal, I was published in the 2017, 2020 FWA Collection volumes, as well as the Florida Writer. I am also published in four "Chicken Soup for the Soul" books.

I became a judge for the RPLA in 2020 and will judge for 2021. I regularly attended FWA writers group meetings and stepped in to lead the River City Writer's group, prior to the pandemic.

Joining the fabulous FWA gave me the confidence I needed to get serious about writing. It provided me with a wonderful group of writers, tools, and resources.

We love living in Florida and I love that the FWA has become my home for writing.

Arielle's Story

by Arielle Haughee
FWA Executive Vice President
FWA Marketing Chair

It was time for a big step. After having a short story published by a speculative fiction magazine, I knew I wanted to dive even further into the world of writing. But I didn't know where to go or who to ask...until I spotted the event calendar for the Maitland Public Library. The Florida Writers Association met once a month and it was the group where the *real* writers were.

But could I fit in with them? Could I make it with the real writers?

I told myself I would hide out in the back row and lay low. The day arrived, and I took a few deep breaths to calm myself. I quietly entered the room. About eight people sat at tables arranged in a U-shape. No back row at all. Rats.

A few more people trickled in, and the leader said the exact words I was dreading: "We're going to go around and say our names and what we write."

I sank in my chair.

"My name is Ken Pelham, and I am the author of..."

He rambled off enough titles to make my head spin.

"Don't forget book of the year!" someone called from the other side of the room.

"Yes, that's right," Ken said with a timid smile. "My book won Published Book of the Year in the Royal Palm Literary Awards."

The leader of the group has to be accomplished, right? Maybe the other folks in the room are newbies like me. Ken gestured for the next attendee to share.

She was a college professor who owned a writing studio and had her own literary magazine.

Yikes. I sank even further. Everyone was sure to laugh me out of the room.

The girl beside me was next. "I'm Kristin Durfee and I'm the author of the Four Corners trilogy." She held up her book. The cover was also printed on her tote bag. "Book two comes out in a few months!"

Everyone clapped.

Then all eyes were on me.

I definitely didn't fit in here. An idea came to me—I could run out of the room. No one knew who I was yet. But running away wouldn't get me anywhere on my writing journey.

The words rushed out of my mouth: "MyNameIsArielleAndIAmNew."

I prepared myself for the imminent laughter.

But that's not what happened.

Instead, a smile grew across Ken's face. "Welcome. We're happy you're here today."

This kindness and community feeling would be the trademark of my experience with FWA for many years to come.

After going to the Maitland Writers Group for a while, I realized I also needed a critique group. Dawn Bell, who published one of my stories, recommended I join her, and the Seminole County Writers Group led by Beda Kantarjian and Joan Levy. I learned volumes from that group and the talented writers there. Beda and Joan also highly encouraged everyone to submit to the Collection and the Royal

Palm Literary Awards. I did not make it into the Collection that year, but I did have quite a surprise coming.

My short story published by Dawn, *Learning to Kick*, won second place for Short Creative Nonfiction. I won an RPLA award!

My confidence soared and I finally felt brave enough to follow my dream. I was a *real* writer.

I was so grateful for the award and the boost it gave me that I wanted to give back to the program. That following RPLA season, I volunteered to be a judge. Chris Coward welcomed me and patiently answered any questions I had. At first, I was incredibly slow, painfully analyzing every single comment I wrote in the rubrics. But I learned to work faster and developed an eye for determining strengths and weaknesses in a story. Being an RPLA judge made me a more thorough critiquer and gave me a better lens to examine my own work.

After submitting two blog posts to Mary Ann de Stefano, I was invited to do the RPLA showcase—a regular blogging position with two to three posts a month featuring the award winners. What fun! I networked with other writers and got to know Mary Ann, who would become a very close friend. My love of blogging blossomed. I did the RPLA showcase for two years, then became a regular blogger.

Then an idea for RPLA formed in my mind. We should have an LGBTQ category.

But I was scared.

How would this new idea be received?

I approached Chris Coward and told her I would do everything necessary to make this happen, contact LGBTQ industry professionals, define the category, and write the rubric. I wasn't sure what I expected, but Chris was not only open, but encouraging. She partnered me with Paul Iasevoli, another person I would come to admire and respect greatly. Paul and I worked tirelessly, going back and forth until we fine-tuned everything as much as we could.

Then I got another surprise. I was invited to the annual RPLA meeting held every January at the same hotel where we do the conference. I couldn't believe my luck. I would get to help with the administration of the competition I loved so much.

Paul and I presented our work to the committee, keeping our fingers crossed. Success! The new category passed with flying colors. I also volunteered to help update a couple other rubrics.

The next RPLA season, I was delighted to be given the position of materials person and the opportunity to dive into something important that needed updating, the RPLA guidelines. New material had been added each year until the guidelines were quite a beast. I spent hour after hour after hour working to simplify them without losing the information. After around forty hours, I cut over ten pages from the guidelines. Phew!

Chris and the others were pleased. Before I knew it, I'd been voted onto the Board of Directors.

Another position would come my way, one that was a bit intimidating, RPLA marketing person.

I was about to step into a new role I wasn't expecting. One I wasn't sure I would be good at...

Everything had been going well with my work for RPLA, even the dreaded marketing. I was swimming along nicely in FWA, enjoying meeting people and the continual kindness and community atmosphere.

Then came a bump in the road.

Our marketing chair, Krys Fenner, had to step down due to other commitments. Once again, all eyes were on me.

I couldn't.

What did I know about marketing?

There was no way I was the right person to steer this ship. But I didn't want to let the organization down, especially after I'd been awarded five RPLAs and made an incredible network. FWA really meant something to me, and I knew in my heart how important it was to support an org that supported me.

So, I said yes.

That's when everything changed when I launched myself full speed into all things FWA.

First on the list, besides all the normal marketing tasks, was to update our logo. I knew it wouldn't be easy to convince the entire board to agree on a design. Should we do an updated version of our old logo or go in a whole new direction? Rick Bettencourt, Mary Ann, and I started a contest on a design site. We selected our top three and presented each of those choices to the board. Funny enough, the three of us each voted for a different choice. They were all so good!

After serious consideration by all board members, we had a winner, "The Wave."

Now for the real work, updating *everything* that had the FWA logo. This included documents, web pages, social media, merchandise, signage, and more. Little by little, we got the job done and our sleek new look was in place.

The fresh logo came with a new marketing approach, really emphasizing what FWA was all about, community. I continued with all things marketing—social media, newsletters, merchandise (hello, Etsy!), ads, graphics, and more—and learned that I truly enjoyed it. FWA believed in me before I believed in myself.

I was on a roll; nothing could stop me!

Then 2020 gave us all the biggest bump in the road we would face, COVID-19.

The decision had been made. Our 2020 conference would pivot to virtual instead of in person. Chrissy Jackson had spent months preparing for our regular event and had to start over. I was so impressed by how quickly she went to Plan B and doubled down on her efforts to make this event succeed.

The problem—none of us knew how to put on a virtual conference.

What platform would we use? How could we have a feeling of community? Would people even want to do it?

Rick, Mary Ann, and I dove headfirst into the tech element, absorbing everything we could about our options and learning on the fly. Chrissy, Paul, Bill Opperman, and Su Gerheim went to work training faculty on the software we chose. Rick set up the framework on Member Click's Learning Management System, embedding video code from Crowd Cast so the sessions would play live on our platform.

I made all the graphics for the site and set up the bells and whistles, the exhibit hall with a sponsor scavenger hunt, the writers' lounge with a chat feature, and the virtual store with presenters' books. Sleep was definitely in short supply during this time.

Finally, it was time to go live.

We didn't have live tech support, so if something went wrong, it was up to Rick, Mary Ann, and I to fix it. We'd set up a help email ahead of time and were going to take turns monitoring it. We tried to send out clear directions, but knew there would be people having trouble. Hopefully it wouldn't be too many.

Ding. An email.

Ding. An email.

Ding. An email.

The three of us scrambled to answer the emails flying in. It was all-hands-on-deck as we frantically emailed and called people to get them into the opening session with Greg Pincus and Robert N. Macomber. I don't think my fingers have ever typed faster. Somehow, some way, we got through it. Everyone who contacted help was able to get into the conference.

The event everyone was looking forward to, the RPLA ceremony, would have two hosts this year to help break up the monotony. My job was to be backup in case Chris Coward or Chris Hamilton's internet went out. I made the slideshow and rehearsed with both of them so there wouldn't be any surprises for me that night.

Or so I thought.

There is something many people don't know about Chris Coward; she can be sneaky when she needs to. A surprise slide appeared when Rick was presenting the President's Award...one with my picture on it! I was completely blown away by the honor and may have shed a tear or two. At that moment, I was quite glad things were virtual and no one could see my blubbering. FWA continued to give back to me, year after year.

So, when an important position opened up, naturally I said yes.

Herb Sennett was finishing his term as EVP and I got a phone call from Rick. Would I be Robin to his Batman? Rick is a skilled leader, able to think logically about things without emotion. I knew with him at the helm, we couldn't go wrong. My term began in January of 2021, and I embraced my new role as well as keeping my marketing chair duties.

I've been able to launch new initiatives including Member of the Month, Member Book of the Month, the Florida Writers Book Expo, our Etsy shop, and special email communication with group leaders. I have even more ideas for future years. I want to preserve the atmosphere of community and always be a "writer helping writers."

Through FWA, I gained confidence in my writing and have made leaps and bounds in my career. I will always be thankful to the organization that welcomed me with open arms and believed in me before I believed in myself, giving me a cape so I could fly ahead in my writing career. I've come a long way since that first Maitland Writers Group meeting and can't wait to see what the future holds for FWA.

Section Two

Annual Florida Writers Conference

Annual Florida Writers Conferences

by Chrissy Jackson
FWA Vice President of Finance
Conference Director

The zenith of every year for the Florida Writers members is the annual conference. The Florida Writers Conference has long been recognized as one of the top writers' conferences in the country, and over the last ten years that reputation has only been enhanced.

Each year, Conference Director Chrissy Jackson scours the country looking for new, timely topics to be presented to members by both new writers and those who are well-established. The National Guest of Honor comes from anywhere in the world, representing the epitome of the genre. The Florida Writer of the Year is another well-known person, bringing their experience to Florida Writers members.

The conference is also a place of tradition with the workshops that are favorites returning year after year: the Gong Show, Open Mic, the special guests interviewing each other, and our Florida Writers Youth Day program.

Authors and faculty have the option to create podcasts which are then stored in the Florida Writers archives and shared. One of our other attractions is the option to book an interview appointment with an agent or editor who is actively acquiring in a particular genre. There are usually seven or more agents/editors at each conference.

The conference bookstore is a busy place, and not only because that's where the beverages are kept, but also because book signings are held throughout the day, and it seems like everyone who comes to the conference takes home at least one new book.

2012 Conference

Among the highlights of the 2012 Conference were an appearance by eleven-year-old author Connor Wilson and his assistant (and father), Jeffrey, wonderful door prizes, and the presentation of the first Kaye Coppersmith Award.

At that year's Florida Writers Foundation Celebrity Workshop, Vic DiGenti delivered a session called "How to Write Killer Fiction". Several dozen people spent the day with Vic, learning secrets for making their novel better than they could possibly dream. This session made for a great start to the conference.

As with every year, the conference features a wide variety of sessions on different topics including Backstory, Parts I and II by Julie Compton and Jamie Morris, Pitch and Catch (on pitching your work) by Ronnie Hart, Behind the Books, a session on juvenile books by Cristina Kessler and Book Marketing Success by Rik Feeney.

15.

There were expert panels, book signings, and opportunities for writers to share their work at Open Mic and prompt-writing sessions. Agents and authors paired off in two different sessions, giving attendees a first-hand look at one of the most important relationships a writer can ever have. There were sessions on point of view, picture books, publishing historical fiction, structuring your fiction, and even writing for Chicken Soup publications.

Each year the FWA President and Vice President recognize someone who has gone above and beyond in serving the organization and helping other writers. This year, for the first time, there was a repeat winner, as Vice President Leona Bodie recognized Mary Ann De Stefano for her hard work maintaining the FWA Network, managing email communications to members, and otherwise improving our online presence. Mary Ann established the FWA's members-only online community (fwanetwork. ning.com) and continues to maintain it.

President Chrissy Jackson recognized Mary Lois Sanders. For the past three years, Mary Lois has worked tirelessly to attract top-flight faculty, agents, and publishers to the conference. In her tenure the quality and scope of the conference sessions had steadily increased, as Mary Lois has consistently strived to provide more quality.

Earlier that year, FWA lost a remarkable woman. Kaye Coppersmith was, for so many people, the soul of the organization, the person who symbolized the motto of writers helping writers. To honor Kaye, the FWA board established the Kaye Coppersmith Award. Nominees were selected by FWA members, and the FWA board selected the winning nominee in a blind vote.

The first Kaye Coppersmith Award went to Palm City Word Weavers leader, Regional Director, and outgoing Vice President Leona Bodie. In both roles, Leona has exemplified what made Kaye special, providing help and information that nurtured all levels of writers, getting speakers for her group, giving guidance and mentoring her follow writers.

The Royal Palm Literary Awards Showcased the best in FWA members' work. Fifty-four selections were named first, second, or third prize winners. The 2012 Published Book of the Year was awarded to *Ordinary People: Extraordinary Heroes* by Will G. Merrill, a history of how ordinary New Yorkers became extraordinary heroes in the first battle of the War against Terror. *The Cold Season* by William C. Walker was named 2012 Unpublished Book of the Year, a woman's journey of discovery and redemption.

2012 FWA Board of Directors

The initial Dahris Clair Memorial Award for Best Screenplay was awarded to *Kidnapped* by Maria Hammarblad. The award is named for former Pasco County group leader Dahris Clair to honor her dedication both to the FWA and to the art of crafting screenplays.

2013 Conference

It was billed as "The Greatest Writers Conference on Earth," and by every measure the 12th Annual Florida Writers Conference lived up to its expectations. Over four hundred attendees filled the Orlando Marriott Lake Mary for a weekend of learning, networking, and inspiration.

Attendees had the opportunity to learn from two talented women. Chantelle Osman, a film consultant, and award-winning mystery writer, conducting a three-hour pre-conference Pitch-Perfect Workshop, designed to help develop and target a pitch, how to pick and find the right agent, and to build confidence.

Mary Burton, "The Queen of Modern-Day Romantic Suspense," presented the 5th Annual Florida Writers Foundation Celebrity Workshop with the topic "Writing Your Book ... Step by Step". The audience in the packed room had a full day to hear Burton speak about the secrets to publishing success.

The Florida Writers Foundation again held a Silent Auction. Attendees bid on prizes donated by sponsors, writers groups, and individuals. In addition, Mary Burton donated the chance to have the winner's name become a character in one of her novels. Proceeds were used to promote literacy.

An annual feature, the Agents and Publishers Panel, attracted a large crowd as industry experts provided a great perspective on the workings of the business. As always, these and other agents and publishers were available for individual sessions giving those interested the opportunity to pitch their work.

There was a presentation of the American flag by a local Boy Scout troop. Michael Wiley, the Person of Renown for *It's a Crime: Florida Writers Association Collection, Volume 5*, was the keynote speaker. He talked about a life of crime writing and the importance of research. In his case, the research got him into some sticky situations, as in the time he stopped to visit a strip club—while his wife and children were in the car. He also managed to visit a massage parlor, all in the name of research and getting the facts right. One of the ten points he outlined to hammer home his point was "Don't write what you know. Learn what you need to know, and then write it." And speaking of hammers, Michael had another story about pounding bullets with a hammer and nail. You had to be there!

The Vice President's Award was given to Susan Berry, and Jim Thompson received the President's Award. Both were honored for their many years of outstanding service to FWA in a variety of roles. They both work tirelessly wherever needed and somehow manage to deliver more than anyone could expect. And what's even more amazing about Susan is that she manages to do all she does for FWA and still finds time to use her husband for target practice.

The Kaye Coppersmith Award, named for our dear friend who passed away in 2012, went to Chrissy Jackson, our outgoing President. Anyone who knows Chrissy knows of her dedication, energy, and drive to make FWA the best organization of its kind, and also her interest in every member, to make sure they get as much from their membership as possible.

The highlight of every annual conference is the Royal Palm Literary Awards banquet. This year, 322 entries were received in twenty-four categories. As the winners were announced, each one walked to the stage to the sound of thunderous applause and cheering. Our motto, "Writers Helping Writers" isn't restricted to learning and improving the craft of writing. It also refers to the support and encouragement we give each other for our success and when we need it to provide a boost to keep pursuing our desire to write.

The major awards were announced to much anticipation. Unpublished Book of the Year went to *Core Pooler* by Dottie Rexford, and Published Book of the Year was given to J. Rivers Hodge for *The Legend of Anne Southern*, an epic novel set during the Civil War. Lastly, the Dahris Clair Award, named for another member who left us too soon, is given to the highest scoring stage play, teleplay, or screenplay. This year it went to *Thornetta: The Musical* by Bridget Callaghan and Jeff Swesky. Congratulations to all the winners and finalists!

2014 Conference

The Florida Writers Conference this year had four New York Times and USA Today bestselling authors, film producers actively seeing material they can adapt into films, medical doctors, and college professors who brought fresh and insightful information to everyone who attended their workshops and panels.

2014 FWA Board of Directors

Not only was the conference filled with the stars of the publishing industry, but the Florida Writers Foundation Celebrity Workshop, sponsored by our sister organization, opened with three dynamic workshops that evening. One of the workshops, "Pitching Your Story," taught by film producers Jillian Stein and Khris Baxter, helped prepare attendees for the pitches they would conduct with agents and acquisition editors all weekend long. Agents like Cathy Watters and Lara Zats, and acquisition editors like Bloomsbury Spark's Meredith Rich, all stated multiple times how delighted they were with the high-level stories pitched to them throughout the weekend. All of them found themselves requesting more manuscripts than they normally request at conferences.

With sometimes as many as four workshops and panels running simultaneously, we made sure to give attendees some guidance on how to choose the right sessions to attend with our new track system. Workshops were scheduled according to one of five tracks—craft, business, genre, writer's life, and panels—and each track catered to writers with different needs.

Craft workshops, such as "Waking from the Comma Coma" and "Mastering the Metaphor," focused on improving the quality of a writer's work overall.

Business workshops, such as "Writing the Query Letter," "How to Sell Books by the Truckload on Amazon," "Using Writing Competitions to Advance Your Career," and "Avoiding the Scams in Self-Publishing," were intended for writers with completed manuscripts who are ready to take the next step with their work.

Genre workshops, such as "World Building" and "Writing Believable New Adult," focused on individual genres, giving writers working within those genres a deeper understanding of the kinds of stories they wanted to tell.

Writers who needed workshops such as "Finding the Work/Life/Writing Balance," "Nutrition for Writers," and "The Idiot's Guide to Networking" found a lot of great information in the Writer's Life track. This track, intended for writers at any stage of their career, was all about making the writer's life healthier, happier, and more creative.

The final track of the conference was the Panel Track. These are workshops in which multiple industry professionals have a chance to weigh in on important questions, so the attendees can be exposed to varied viewpoints on the same topics. We brought four brand new panels to the Florida Writers Conference this year.

Friday night's "Writing About Sex" panel dove into the intricacies of romance and erotica, studying the importance of sexual tension over the physical acts of sex. With a "bring your own wine" policy, this panel was a lot of fun and one of the most popular at the conference.

Saturday's "It's Time to Diversify" panel explored Transmedia Writing and the importance of writing in more than one format. The writers represented on this panel work in novels, short stories, games, comics, graphic novels, films, television, children's books, and more!

Finally, our twin panels of "Publishing with an Agent" and "Publishing Without an Agent" explored the two paths an author can choose between. "With an Agent" focused on the process of getting published after a writer has secured an agent, exploring what an agent's job is like and the timeline it takes for a book to sell. "Without an Agent" looked at the various paths available to the unrepresented writer, from self-publishing to submitting to a small or digital press.

For the first time, we encouraged writers attending the conference to use Twitter to help document their experience. Needless to say, #FWA2014 got a *lot* of attention over the weekend. Compliments were shared about the stellar faculty and the fantastic hotel staff. Friends were made and accomplishments were shared. Writers used this amazing social media tool to share their reactions to pitches, sessions, people, and their conference experience overall.

Several sessions were even "live tweeted," which means that attendees continued to tweet throughout a panel or workshop, sharing the valuable knowledge they learned with the world at large. It's because of this combined effort to share knowledge that #FWA2014 went viral over the weekend, bringing worldwide attention to our conference.

The highlight of the Annual Florida Writers Conference is always the Royal Palm Literary Awards Banquet and Ceremony. With our Hollywood-style theme of "The Starts of the Florida Writers," attendees gathered in tiaras and boas and filled out their clapboard centerpieces to celebrate the accomplishments of their fellow members.

Dozens of awards were given out in both Published and "Pre-Published" categories, but there were three big winners of the night. The Published Book of the Year Award went to *Deadly Drifts* by MW Gordon, and the Pre-Published Book of the Year Award went to *Sacred Ashes* by Lloyd R. Agee.

Finally, the Dahris Clair Memorial Award went to the screenplay *The Silver Bullet*, written by Jennie Jarvis.

2015 Conference

The weekend's events fell in several tracks, including Craft Considerations, Business Details, Genre Specific Topics, Technology Usage, and the Writer's Life. This year the best presentations of the FWA Mini-Conferences were invited to the annual conference for an encore. In addition, the conference featured several special events, including the annual Florida Writers Foundation Celebrity Workshop with John Gilstrap, an immersive "Be a Real CSI for a Day!" workshop, and a Youth Writers Conference. From the nuts and bolts of how to avoid bad grammar, strategies for writing series and building suspense, utilizing various points of view, formatting dialogue, utilizing tropes, and incorporating imagery, to more global considerations such as character development, antagonist's story arcs, and the fundamentals of comedic and tragic storytelling, the conference faculty shared their subject-area expertise to help writers improve their storytelling.

The Gong Show Pitch Fest, back by popular demand, featured a panel of agents, editors, and film producers listening and critiquing any attendee brave enough to say their pitch in a room full of other writers. Many panels covered the basics of contract negotiation, publishing with or without an agent, small press publishing, and self-publication.

Workshops covered important topics such as how to pitch and network, your publication options, how to print your own books, options for actually making money as a writer, effectively marketing your writing by offering swag, and avoiding publishing scams. Several open-ended workshops and panels were offered as well, where attendees could ask agents, attorneys, and editors whatever questions they may have had. The most anticipated workshop, "How I Sold Over 150,000 Books on Amazon," covered the secrets to one local writer's stunning success.

A panel about writing for youth covered several age ranges from picture books to chapter novels, while a Story to Screen panel discussed the adaptation process and how screenplays come to life. This year's conference featured three panels about poetry (including how to market it!) and several panels on research, especially regarding fact-checking for religious characters, historical fiction, sports writing, science in science fiction, and military technical details. Specific genre-specific craft considerations, such as those needed in romance writing, horror, and suspense were covered, as well as workshops on the specifics of screenwriting, short writing, flash fiction, and novellas.

Regardless of where the attendees fell on the spectrum of tech-savvy to not-so-much, this conference offered something for everyone. Workshops included introductions to writing software like Final Draft, Scrivener, or Prowriting Aid, how to self-market smarter by making book trailers and using Twitter, and even covering Photoshop usage for book jacket design.

In addition to star-studded panels discussing different writer's writing processes and the pros and cons of attending a creative writing Master of Fine Arts program, several workshops covered topics such as how to get the most out of your conference experience, how to present yourself at readings, how to channel stress productively, using meditation and freewriting to create new work, where to find writing challenges to write all year long, what it's like to be a Hollywood writer, and how to submit your work to literary journals for publication.

A day-long seminar, Florida Writers Foundation Celebrity Workshop: Adrenaline Rush: How to Write Suspense Fiction, highlighted the key elements needed to write effective and intelligent suspense fiction. John Gilstrap utilized a combination of lecturing and writing exercises to cover topics including plot construction, character development, and story structure, giving attendees a window into the underlying organization of riveting page-turners.

Crime Scene Investigator Sharon L. Plotkin taught a day-long hands-on workshop unveiling the truths of crime investigation in real life, utilizing the real terminology and equipment used in the field. In addition to learning about blood splatter analysis, luminol, ballistics, and arson, attendees took home a massive, full-color booklet of reference materials.

A single-day Youth Writers Conference provided younger writers with great writing tips and tricks for multiple genres and mediums of storytelling, advice on essential workshopping techniques, and even strategies for achieving publication, all taught by the same talented faculty featured in the main conference.

The Florida Writers Conference would not be complete without the prestigious Royal Palm Literary Awards Banquet. These awards highlighted writers across multiple genres and mediums, including book-length fiction and nonfiction, whole works, poetry, screenplays, and more.

In addition to all of these wonderful workshops, panels, and events, what really makes the Florida Writers Conference stand out is the commitment of its members and attendees to uphold the Florida Writers Association motto: Writers Helping Writers. This conference featured countless opportunities for attendees to network and get to know one another. In addition to the signature Genre Breakfasts, which give attendees an opportunity to meet other writers who compose in the same genre(s), this year featured a Friday night Open Mic opportunity for members to share their own work and hear from others.

The conference bookstore housed the esteemed works of faculty presenters and FWA members, and the silent auction's offerings were some of the best. Attendees participated in book signings and signed up for interviews with agents, editors, filmmakers, and authors as well as manuscript critiques by industry experts.

2016 Conference

Tosca Lee, author of megahits including *The Progeny*, blitzes attendees with an all-day workshop on her ten secrets of achieving bestseller status. The Annual Celebrity Workshop, which raises funds to promote literacy in the state of Florida, was sponsored by the Florida Writers Foundation.

Two talented souls—Elaine Person with poetry prompts, and Melissa Gibbo with fiction writing prompts—present Early Bird Workshops. Sharon Plotkin hosts an all-day forensics workshop, "To Catch a Killer." It's hands-on and hands-dirty, with a mock crime scene and working crime scene lab.

Authors selected for Florida Writers Association Collection

That year's FWA Person of Renown and International Man of Mystery, John Gilstrap (author of International Thriller Writers 2016 Best Paperback Original, *Against All Enemies*), gives a shout-out to authors of the latest FWA collection, Hide & Seek.

Tasked with reviewing all the stories, he raves about the quality of the writing and the production values. John has ranked his top ten, tabbing Chris Hamilton's *Can I Help You with That* as his number one pick. High praise indeed.

Gilstrap is also the keynote speaker, and he makes it both personal and universal. "Be aware of serendipity," he says. "Stuff happens. Deal with it, go with it. Stuff works out. You have no idea what the future holds so grab the bull by the horns and hold on tight. Cowboy up!" he demands.

The conference held a demonstration on putting on Facebook events—launch parties and the like—by FWA's resident social media mavens. The Youth Writers take center stage with Youth Writers RPLA. So many great writers of the future, and the Candice Coghill Award for the highest scoring entry goes to Sarina Patel for her poem *She Comes Home*. The future of American literature is bright.

On to the awards, the heart of the matter. Recognizing tireless dedication to the cause, Chrissy Jackson announced this year's Kaye Coppersmith Award winner, Chris Coward, the President's Award winner, Robyn Weinbaum, and the Vice President's Award winner, Mary Lois Sanders.

The number of RPLA entries continues to grow each year. In 2015, 393 entered. This year there were a whopping 479, a 22% increase. To handle the workload, the number of judges rose to 168, up from 125 last year. Chris Coward gives a rundown of changes in the judging criteria, thanks the judges for their hard work, asks them to stand, and launches into a list of impressive works and writers.

Throughout the calls to the stage to award recipients, reactions range from shock to elation. Highlighting the event, runners-up, and winners of the three highest honors share the spotlight, with Bill Dougherty taking home the Dahris Clair Memorial Award for his screenplay, *Shinyo Maru*, Jennifer Boddicker winning Unpublished Book of the Year for her mainstream/literary novel,

Cleaning House, and E.J. Wenstrom taking Published Book of the Year for her fantasy novel, *Mud*.

2017 Conference

The Florida Writers Foundation kicked things off with a separate and signature event, NYT best-selling thriller writer David Morrell's celebrity workshop, "Lessons from a Lifetime of Writing." Morrell spoke of passion, the key to all the projects. If he isn't passionate about something he is writing, he explains, it really isn't worth his time. There has to be a core to the book, something that would involve him completely. No passion, no core. Sage advice.

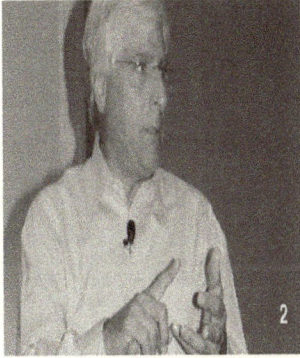

E.J. Wenstrom, 2016's Published Book of the Year winner for her spellbinding fantasy novel, *Mud*, spoke about this year's FWA collection, *What a Character!* A panel of five talented authors, Doug Dandridge, Micki Browning, Carla Norton, Dan Alatorre, and Nancy J. Cohen presented a panel on "Dredging Up Your Dark Side."

Guest appearances at the reception by Superman, Supergirl, and Wonder Woman brought smiles and an unprecedented level of security to the hotel. They took time from saving the world and whatnot to pose for pictures with eager conference-goers, and word out on the street was that David Morrell was drafted into the Justice League by the three superheroes.

Steve Berry, FWA's Florida Writer of the Year, was the keynote speaker. Like many writers, he had accumulated a stock of unpublished manuscripts, but knew with each effort that he continued to improve. In spite of the urge to hang it all up, the little voice kept him going. "Writers aren't born," he says, in his velvet Southern accent. "The little voices inside our heads are the voices that won't let us quit."

In the years I've attended the conference, the difference between Friday and Saturday is astonishing. The place gets packed with attendees early, and the place is really hopping. There's also something about the genre-breakfasts which settles us in. Acquaintances are made over coffee, and old acquaintances become friends. More attendees arrive, and soon everyone is cramming workshops in by the bushel. The workshops are running at a pace of seven simultaneously throughout the day. It's an embarrassment of riches, but so difficult to pick and choose.

There were winners in twenty-six categories of the Royal Palm Literary Awards, with Debbie Reed Fischer winning Best Children's Book for *This is Not the Abby Show*. For Unpublished Book of the Year, runners-up were Kimberlee Esselstrom, Caroline Tillotson, and Patricia Crumpler, with Karen Dillon winning for her historical novel, *On a Winter Shore*. For Published Book of the Year, the runners up were Jack L. Hayes, Phyllis Smallman, Carol J. Post, and Doug Alderson, with Jim Pons taking the top honor for his memoir, *Hard Core Love*. Mention is made of Jim's stints as bass player with 1960s bands The Leaves, The Turtles, and Frank Zappa's Mothers of Invention.

2018 Conference

The Conference theme of "Where Does Your Muse Live" reflected the abundance of inspiration, education, and motivation stuffed into three-and-a-half days of non-stop action.

Heather Graham, Florida Writer of the Year; Vic DiGenti, Conference Faculty Chair; Linda Fairstein, National Guest of Honor; and Peter Meinke, Poet Laureate of Florida.

Chuck Sambuchino, during his Celebrity Workshop, immediately demonstrated his total grasp of the subject matter, speaking without notes, answering questions, and even critiquing queries and first pages.

Linda Fairstein was the National Guest of Honor, and Heather Graham was the Florida Writer of the Year for the 2018 conference. They then settled into comfortable armchairs on that Friday for a one-on-one interview, with Heather asking the questions, and Linda revealing insights into her life and career. The former sex crimes prosecutor regaled us with anecdotes from her 29-year career with the New York County DA's office, and how she had always wanted to be a mystery writer. The tables were turned on Saturday morning when the prosecutor interviewed witness Heather Graham. The authors are good friends and displayed a keen sense of humor, entertaining the audience with many stories of the writing life.

Six concurrent hourly sessions covered fiction and nonfiction, a smattering of technology, a lot of marketing and business, and most tracks also contained a panel discussion.

During the Collection Luncheon, we heard from the "Person of Renown," the winner of the 2017 Book of the Year author Jim Pons, who had the unenviable duty of selecting his top ten favorite entries from the sixty winning Collections book stories. Jim had a remarkable life, which he documented in his memoir, *Hard Core Love*. He also proved to be an effective speaker.

Thanks to the generosity of our two special guest authors, we were able to auction off the opportunity to have the highest bidder's character name used in a future novel or story. Toward the end of Friday's luncheon there was spirited bidding and the high bidder's name will soon be immortalized in one of Heather Graham's books. We repeated the auction at Saturday evening's dinner for a character name in a future Linda Fairstein book. Altogether, we raised $1,700 for the Florida Writers Foundation. Heather Graham presented a two-hour workshop Friday afternoon that gave all in attendance the chance to write their own short story. She started with a one-sentence prompt, "She lay in a pool of blood." Each person had been given slips of paper containing a noun and a verb describing a character. For example, grubby and ballet dancer. They then had to use that character to write their story. Heather offered advice throughout, and then allowed the writers to read their stories. Great fun that proved we have many impressive writers in our membership.

National Guest of Honor Linda Fairstein mesmerized the crowd at Friday night's Welcome Dinner with tales of her life as a lawyer, prosecutor, and author. One of the highlights was her closing story about having lunch with Harvey Weinstein. It was a funny story with a surprising twist at the end. You had to have been there.

More people arrived on Saturday and packed the halls and meeting rooms. After breakfast, Heather Graham was interviewed, and we learned about her many charitable causes, like Writers for New Orleans, and the Romantic Times Vampire Ball, which raises money for a children's charity. She also admitted she had no idea how many books she's written, but it had to be in the hundreds.

Saturday was also the day for FWAY, the Florida Writers Association Youth Conference, and Mark Newhouse and Kristen Stieffel did an amazing job organizing the event. The spotlight was on the young writers at lunch, as FWA honored the winners of the Youth RPLA competition, and those who made it into the Youth Collection book. Watching these young writers come forward to be recognized was heart-warming for this old writer. Announcements of the annual Vice President's and President's Awards followed, giving recognition to two stalwart FWA volunteers, Anne Dalton, and Rick Bettencourt, respectively.

The highlight of every conference is Saturday evening's Royal Palm Literary Awards Banquet, and this one topped them all. A lovely young Genie roamed the exhibition space, offering glammed-up attendees the opportunity to rub a magic lamp. From the moment we walked in the room it was obvious this would be an enchanted night, with the softly glowing centerpieces and the sounds of a sitar in the background.

As always, RPLA Chair Chris Coward did an amazing job moving the evening along, announcing the many winners, which culminated in the Published Book of the Year, whose author would be the 2019 Person of Renown. Retired police captain Micki Browning's mystery novel, *Beached*, took that honor, a return to the podium for Micki, since her first book, *Adrift*, won the 2015 RPLA Unpublished Book of the Year.

2019 Writers Conference

There was no shortage of industry professional at this conference. With six literary agents, two acquisition editors, and dozens of presenters, the knowledge and opportunities were flowing. National Guest of Honor Jonathan Maberry "spent the entire weekend educating and entertaining attendees," said Melody Dimick, President of the Florida Writers Foundation. "He passed on a variety of information about the art of the pitch. There was never a dull moment all day. High energy," Barry Dimick added.

Another National Guest of Honor, Sherrilyn Kenyon, had the crowd in stitches talking about a "teleporting cat" that caused her foot injury. Her lively humor made for invigorating discussion about story content, pen names, marketing, and use of the term "horror." Florida Writer of the Year Delilah S. Dawson wowed the audience with her knowledge on fantastic first pages and words of encouragement for new writers or anyone facing challenges in their writing journey.

Seasoned authors were delighted to find a variety of advanced sessions such as ad strategies for Facebook

marketing, exploring copyright issues, and audio production. Workshops on trending subgenres, including ret-
ropunk, erotica, and rhyming poetry encouraged writers
to explore something new. Several sessions focused on
featuring diversity in stories in authentic ways. Classic
writing craft mainstays had a place as well, plotting, characters, setting, dialogue, and many more. Overall, there
was something for everyone at the 2019 conference.

Another fantastic highlight was the faculty interview
sessions. Attendees could sign up for a time slot to share
their work with an industry professional of their choice.

Another great stop at the conference was the silent auction benefitting the Florida Writers Foundation. Baskets
overflowing with goodies filled the tables. Everything
from signed books to Amazon gift cards to bottles of wine
to event tickets. The basket donor who receives the highest
bid gets a prize each year. This year Mark Newhouse and
his group "Writers 4 Kids" won a taco party for earning
the highest donation. Enjoy those tacos, crew!

Florida Youth Writers Conference attendees joined
adult members for lunch on Saturday and enjoyed the
cheers and applause as youth winners of the Royal

Palm Literary and FWA Collection competitions were recognized.

2020 Remote Conference

Because of the COVID-19 Pandemic, holding the 2020 Conference proved to be the most challenging in the history of the Florida Writers Association. "Never did we consider cancelling the event!" declared Chrissy Jackson. As a result, the conference was held virtually for the first time from October 15-18. "While we consider the opportunity to attend the annual conference an FWA membership benefit, we also consider providing it an FWA leadership requirement," noted Jackson, the Conference Chair for the fifteenth time.

By midyear, the planners decided the live event would not be possible.

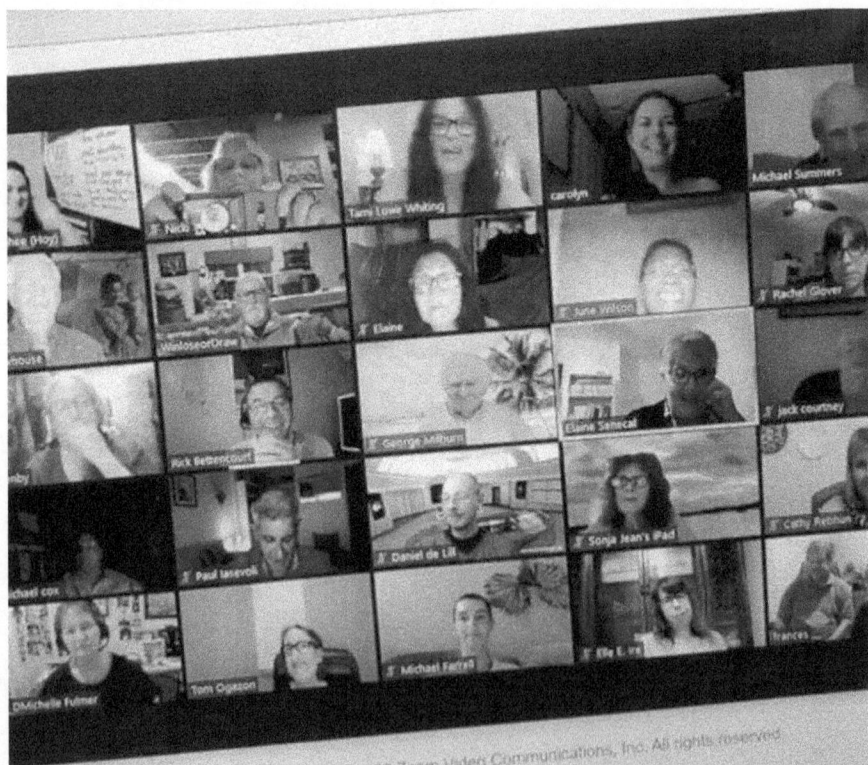

A small army of volunteers stepped up and met the challenge to create an online platform, train staff in the technology, moderate sessions, provide technical support to attendees throughout the conference, and market the new-to-us remote event.

While there may have been some concern about member reaction, response was good, nearly 400 people registered for the conference, and some of those registrations might have represented more than a single participant.

The theme of the conference, "Create an Illusion," was captured perfectly by jets of bright color blasting from an open computer screen as the conference kicked off with a Thursday evening conversation between two high-profile guests, Greg Pincus and Robert N. Macomber. Pincus, the writer of the film "Little Big League" and the middle-grade novel *The Homework Strike*, was the 2020 conference's National Guest of Honor. Macomber, author of the *Honor* series of historical novels was the 2020 Florida Writer of the Year.

Pincus and Macomber presented a congenial hour of wit and helpful advice that set the tone for the rest of the weekend. Among the nuggets offered by Macomber and Pincus:

- Beware of story-stoppers. Macomber recommended vulgarities, excessively grisly descriptions, and the like, can jar a modern audience by being out of place in the historical setting.
- Pincus enjoined us to respect our audience's plausibility limits. For instance, in *Little Big League* the major premise was that a kid inherited a Major League Baseball team and appointed himself team manager. A terrific kernel for a fun tale, but let's face it, not very realistic. For that very reason, Pincus took great pains that the rest of the story should ring very true-to-life.

- Sometimes the painfulness of research can be a blessing in disguise, Macomber advised. After all, how can you describe the cooking smells on the streets of Cartagena, Colombia, unless you travel there and experience them for yourself? Oh, and the trip, properly managed, might be a tax-deduction opportunity!

Panel discussions and instruction presentations filled the rest of the weekend. Though these offerings were not as numerous as at previous conferences, the quality and variety were first rate. Four agents convened on the topic "Query Letters That Work!" and Nancy J. Cohen shared secrets on increasing your audience with Audiobooks. Point of view issues while writing fiction, writing non-fiction through a fiction lens, using color to make your poetry come to life, and features of the Scrivener software package were among the other topics covered by sessions available to attendees.

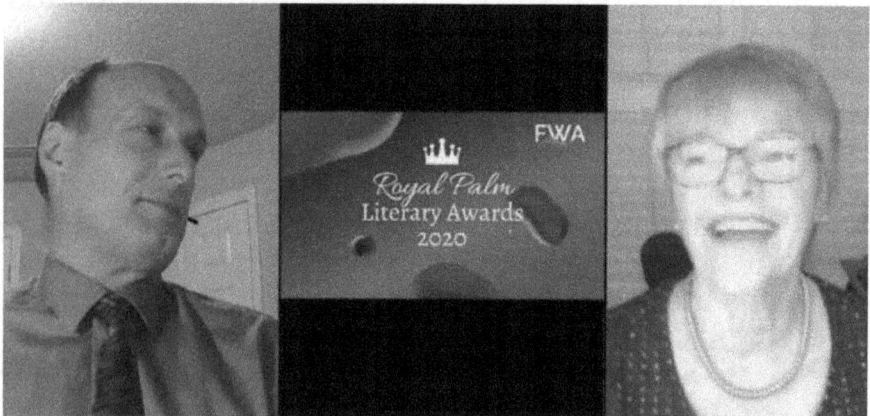

Saturday evening was dedicated to the Royal Palm Literary Awards ceremony. Chris Coward and Chris Hamilton shared announcer duties for the majority of the awards, occasionally yielding the spotlight to appropriate special guests, Mark Newhouse, the chairperson of FWAY, the Florida Writers Association Youth Program, was tapped to present the Candice Coghill Award for the best Youth entry to Jacqueline Cook for her poem *Blue and Black*. Executive Vice President Herb Sennett presented the Vice President's Award to Chrissy Jackson, and President Rick Bettencourt named Arielle Haughee recipient of the President's Award.

Chrissy Jackson was called upon to announce the winner of the Kaye Coppersmith Award. This very special award recognizes that member who best exemplifies the FWA motto: Writers Helping Writers. Nominations are made by members who prepare written tributes for the nominees. These testimonials are then judged blind by the FWA Directors. This year the Kaye Coppersmith Award was conferred upon Beda Kantarjian.

An exciting new program was announced in conjunction with the final award, the most prestigious award for writing of the evening. The Omega Project has recently been established by Lifetime FWA member David Harding in honor of his late wife, Kathryn DePumpo Harding, an ardent supporter of Florida Writers over the years. Fifty volunteers have received a check for $25.00 from the Omega Project and have committed to purchase, read, and honestly review the Published Book of the Year, in this case, *The Orphan of Pitigliano* by Marina Brown. The object is to help launch our premier author's effort.

One of the features of this virtual conference was the opportunity for repeated viewings of the sessions if we want to take notes or simply enjoy them again. The offerings remained available on the conference website until November 15.

Section Three

Royal Palm Literary Awards Competition

Royal Palm Literary Awards Competition

by Chris Coward
Royal Palm Literary Awards Chair

So, you want to be an award-winning author. Or maybe you want anonymous feedback to up your writing game. Or both. Maybe you're going after the holy grail: selling millions of books like J.K. Rowling, Agatha Christie, Barbara Cartland, Harold Robbins, or Dr. Seuss. Or that other holy grail: writing something so profound that your work becomes a classic, and future students are required to read it.

The very year FWA was founded, the Royal Palm Literary Awards (RPLA) competition was established to address all of these needs.

With so many writing competitions out there, what makes RPLA special? Count multifaceted goals as one huge differentiator, as described in the RPLA mission statement:

"The Royal Palm Literary Awards competition is a service of the Florida Writers Association established to recognize excellence in members' published and unpublished works while providing objective and constructive written assessments for all entrants."

It's quite simple, actually. FWA was founded on the principle of Writers Helping Writers, and for the past twenty years, RPLA has embraced that mindset. Although RPLA is a writing competition, more than anything, it was intended to help writers at all stages of their writing journey improve their craft and achieve their dreams.

Crucial in achieving that goal is feedback in the form of rubrics, where all entrants receive their scores and comments from multiple judges using a variety of genre-specific criteria.

Like many new initiatives, RPLA started modestly. When I took on the chairmanship in 2008, I started with the names of eleven judges, a few rough rubric templates, and a trickle of entries. Over the years the team has built up the competition, and in 2020, boasted some 160 judges, 59 different rubrics, and 542 entries.

A few milestones since 2011:

- Creating a system for discrepancy judging should initial judge scores diverge fifteen or more points
- Adding rubric coordinators to review the rubrics and serve as an added layer for quality control
- Adding a process to notify entrants of the status of their entries throughout the competition
- Adding a youth component
- Upgrading the awards banquet to include a continuous-loop finalist slide show, winners' slide show, and grand prizes
- Creating badges for semifinalists, finalists, winners, and grand winners to display in their email signature fields, on their websites, on social media, on their book covers, and on general marketing pieces
- Adding judge training in the form of judge packets, three videos, and sample rubrics

As a result, RPLA has become a cornerstone of FWA's culture. Every year, we see FWA writing groups support their member's entry efforts, not only by critiquing the drafts before submission but also by cheering finalists on at the awards ceremony. The ceremonies themselves never lack for warm moments, many bittersweet. One year, a friend accepted a trophy for a winner in the hospital. Another year, a winner's daughter accepted the trophy on behalf of her mother, who passed away a month before the ceremony—before she knew she'd won. These are only two of many moist-eye moments in RPLA's history.

There's no shortage of stories from entrants who credit RPLA for giving them confidence and in some cases, making it possible for them to acquire an agent or publisher. More importantly, there's no shortage of stories from entrants who thank the team for rubrics that enabled them to move to the next level.

Recent testimonials:

"Because of this amazing contest, I recently signed with Levine Greenberg Rostan Literary!!! Home of *Gone, Girl*, ya'll. This past contest was a life changer."

—*Melissa Abrehamsen*

"Three different categories and the responses were awesome! It is such an economic bargain to submit to the RPLA! The knowledge and thoughtfulness of all the judges blew me away. Now that I know more about writing, I can appreciate the depth, time, and attention that were given by all eight judges. Wow!! ... I have also found that when I returned to the rubric responses that stung at bit, usually the remarks were correct. It just took me some time to get to the point that I could see it."

—*Margarita McCarthy w/a Elena Fowler*

"The rubrics may be the very best part of the contests. It is inspiring that so many writers step up to the
bar to contribute their knowledge and views. Thank you!
Thank you!"

—*Joan Harris*

"These rubrics were just so helpful—and it shows such
a high level of judging with such time and effort put into
each work."

—*Marty Ambrose*

"Yours is the only writing organization to which I
belong that gives this helpful feedback."

—*Dr. Ruth Baskerville*

"They are the best feedback I have received to date on
my writing—so clear, so honest."

—*David Mather*

"Very professional and validating—thank you."

—*Sonja Mongar*

In twenty years, RPLA has gained exponentially in
prestige and in usefulness to FWA members. Our goal is
to continue on that trajectory.

Section Four

FWA Collection Contests

FWA Collection Contests

The member benefit called FWA Collection Contest was a young three-year-old event when the Florida Writers Association celebrated its 10th Anniversary in 2011. The idea came to fruition in 2009 at an afternoon get-together between Chrissy Jackson and Kaye Coppersmith. They wanted to stimulate writing, challenge creativity, and give the then 850 members a reward that would boost writing journeys for both experienced and new writers.

Chrissy and Kaye, the contest architects, created an original structure that has remained intact since day one. A published book containing sixty winning stories, written against a theme, featuring a Person of Renown (POR) who would rank their top ten favorites. Each year would have a new theme and a new POR. Guidelines were established and the first FWA Collection Contest, Volume One, *From Our House to Yours*, was published in 2009 featuring POR Suzette Martinez Standring.

At the start, members could submit as many entries as they wished with no more than two winning stories per author being published. The contest was a tremendous success. Entries boomed and in three years the need for two changes become apparent. The first was to limit submissions to no more than

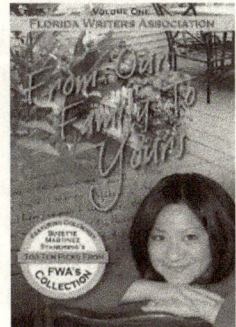

two per author. The second was to limit the number of entries published to one per author. This worked well and entries continued to increase.

In 2013 the FWA added a special book signing event at the annual conference for the winning authors in the collection contest. Coupled with a conference group picture, the event raised the excitement for attendees who purchased a record 438 books.

Another change that same year allowed poetry submissions into the contest. Volume Five, *It's A Crime!* with POR Michael Wiley, saw the highest member participation in its history with 176 authors submitting 231 entries. Not entirely surprising, since the popular writing genres, crime, mystery, suspense, and thriller all fell within that theme. It was an exciting time with more innovations yet to come.

One year later, 2014, for Volume Six, *The First Step*, with POR Mary Burton, technology changed the face of the Collection contest. All submissions went to a digital form posted to the Florida Writers Association website and a FAQs section was added to the guidelines to make the digital process more user friendly. Over time, this reduced emails flying back and forth between entrants and the administration team.

A huge innovation, also occurring in 2014, was the addition of youth writers to the contest. The collection administration team had been brainstorming ways our youth writers could participate. The result was the creation of a spin-off of the Collection contest specifically tailored to youth. The theme and POR would be the same, but the winners would be included in the current year's volume until enough youth participation enabled publication of their own, separate Collection book with sixty winning youth authors. It was quickly discovered that youth writers especially enjoyed writing poetry. Their contest is now in its eighth year and going strong.

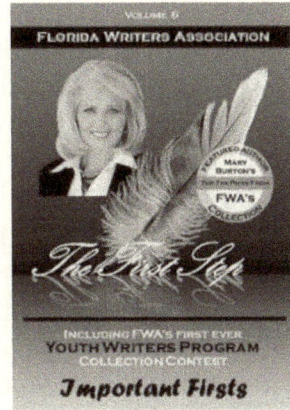

Every year improvements suggested by participants as well as initiated by industry standards are taken into consideration. The administrative team is open to all ideas that enhance the value of the contest for our writing community.

With that in mind, one the of greatest improvements came with Volume Nine, *What a Character!* It was decided to invite the FWA Royal Palm Literary Award (RPLA) winner for Published Book of the Year to be the featured Person of Renown for the following year's Collection contest book.

In 2017, that POR was EJ Wenstrom, the 2016 RPLA Published Book of the Year award winner with her novel titled *Mud*. Then came the Collection contest's 10th Anniversary. With that volume, titled *Where Does Your Muse Live?* published in 2018, the number of published winners was increased to seventy-five to celebrate the occasion. Not surprisingly, the books usual yearly printing of 500 for distribution soared to 625, with sales of 615, subsequently becoming the highest in the contest's history.

In 2020, Volume Twelve, *Create an Illusion*, with POR Mark H. Newhouse, was undoubtedly the most challenging year for all of Florida Writers Association with the onslaught of the COVID-19 virus. It meant, in a matter of months, our writing community had to learn how to produce an annual conference remotely via computers. In terms of the annual conference, many opportunities had to be redesigned, recorded and/or reduced. For the Collection contest the book-signing event and group picture had to go, and the celebration of Collection winners at the annual conference had to be recorded. It was a strange experience, announcing and showing pictures of winners, but not hearing or seeing their cheers, clapping, and noisy jumping up and down.

Now in its thirteenth year, the Collection contest celebrates Florida Writers Association's 20th Anniversary. The theme for the contest is footprints. The collection contest team looks forward to a future filled with continued volumes of exciting books from a diverse, talented writing community.

Section Five

Florida Writers Foundation
Silent Auction

Florida Writers Foundation Silent Auction

by Tami Lowe Whiting
FWA Silent Auction Chair

THE HEART IS...YOU

The Body...

In January 2019, as the new Silent Auction Chair, I attended the FWA WRAP meetings, to go over what worked at the 2018 Conference, and what could be improved. The volunteers sat in a rectangle: RPLA, Interviews, The Collections, Registration, Sponsors, FWAY, the Photographer, Podcast, Volunteers, Faculty, the RPLA Banquet and the Bookstore. It was fascinating to see how the machine-body functioned. I was impressed and admired their choices to serve our community of writers.

I stayed the next day to attend the Foundation's board meeting. I wasn't really sure what the Florida Writers Foundation was, or that it was different from the Association. The separateness became clearer with the discussions we had that day and in the coming months.

We also squeezed in a separate meeting to orient me to the FWF Silent Auction. Susan Boyd, the She-God of Auctions, had prepared step-by-step instructions for me, as well as the leaders of FWA and FWF. I took notes and absorbed while my heart rate and cortisol levels increased. What was I doing? And why was I doing it?

Best Conference Ever...

I'd attended the FWA conference twice, and a couple of minis, as an Enjoyer. I swam in the sea of knowledge and efforts of others I was completely unaware of. I much preferred FWA to the AWP, and even the Sanibel Island Writers Conference. The word WARMTH has been used several times to describe the difference with our conference, and I agree.

The process of prepping the Auction started in April. Each new step brought stress and fear that my efforts would not be good enough. Vulnerability was my teacher. Each bullet that I checked on Susan's list gave me incrementally more confidence.

Thank Yous...

If you attended the 18th Annual Florida Writers Conference in October, we thank you. If you attended the FWF Celebrity Workshop, we thank you. Thank you for your smiles and conversations and for teaching me what you learned in workshops while we ate breakfast together.

Thank you for perusing our Silent Auction room and thank you for bidding on items.

Thank you so much to all those who donated items. We had some great things, some of which I couldn't help bidding on myself. I'm thoroughly enjoying my Kindle Fire HD 8 with cover and Amazon card from Taylor and Seale Publishing.

Much thanks to Barbara Meyers and Susan Boyd for helping to run EVERYTHING smoothly, and our other volunteers during the weekend.

Success!

The Foundation received seventy-three auction items. Sixteen of these were from FWA Writing Groups! Thank you so much. The FWA Writing Group that brought in the highest bid and won the coveted Taco Party reward was Writers 4 Kids from The Villages.

Twenty-one donations were experiences from Florida companies, for which we are incredibly grateful. Many companies have chiseled their policies of giving to non-profits, so we were happy to receive these. The remaining thirty-six donations were from conference faculty, authors, publishers, editors, agents, and other writing groups. I appreciate you all so very much.

Where the FWF Money Goes...

We currently sponsor the publication, Cross Creek Chronicle, a compilation of student and teacher writing of Pinellas County Elementary Schools. In the Palm Beach area, we are sponsoring an Essay Writing Challenge in middle and high schools. We also sponsor an Anthology at the inspiring Chiles Academy in Daytona Beach, which educates and empowers teen mothers. We are considering other grant proposals for 2020.

The Heart of the FWA and FWF...

None of this matters without you. All of these moving parts that create what I believe to be the best writer's conference mean nothing without all of you who attend the FWA Conference and donate to the FWF. The entire machine is volunteer based. Right now, it's my turn to work. One of these years, I'll pass the baton to someone who is ready, but maybe doesn't know it. Then I will once again be an Enjoyer, bustling to workshops and taking notes.

Follow Us...

If you haven't already done so, go to Facebook and find the Florida Writers Foundation group AND the Florida Writers Foundation, INC page—that's where the magic will happen. Additionally, follow us on Instagram at Florida Writers Foundation and Twitter at FloridaWritersFoundation (@WritersFlorida). We'll post details and, of course, see you at the Silent Auction.

Testimonial from The FWF Auction Room.

Humor me while I assume that you, dear reader, have never been to see me at the Florida Writers Conference at the Hilton in North Orlando, Altamonte Springs. I'm not offended at your never entering through my door, but perhaps you'll let me attempt to tempt you to stop in this fall?

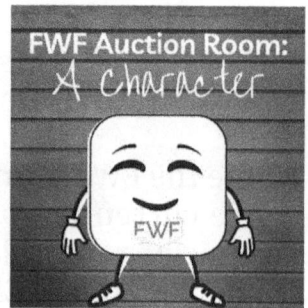

FWF Auction Room: A character

I have a neutral, typical hotel door wearing a sandwich sign with my open times. My door is heavy but kept open just for you. Twinkle lights greet your eyes just a few feet ahead. You must take three steps to touch them. The warm lights continue across a line of tables, skirting my perimeter, first red, and then green and finally white. I'm also wearing tablecloths in matching colors. I am decorated for a holiday shopping aesthetic, and I look amazing.

This is perhaps one of my favorite events all year. Why, you wonder?

Preparation for this event starts back in May. My helpers request donations from generous companies, conference faculty, and FWA Writing Group Leaders for months in advance. Spreadsheets are created, filled, and filed. Displays are well-planned and intentional.

They plan ahead to take great care of me because I provide the perfect fundraising storm—supplying grant money for literacy programs in your Florida neighborhoods. That's what the Florida Writers Foundation is all about.

My money funds an anthology at Chiles Academy in Daytona Beach, a school serving "any pregnant or parenting teen in Volusia County from grades 6 through 12," because all of humanity deserves an education with reading and writing at its base.

My money funds "1000 Books before Kindergarten" at W.T. Bland Library in Mount Dora, promoting reading from infancy to age five and growing children's home libraries, believing that every child should own a book.

My money has funded essay writing contests in middle and high schools, and therapy reading dogs at libraries.

When I think about the little time I give hosting this worthy fundraiser, getting all dressed up to be enticing, I feel proud and thoroughly blissed. I am doing something to help. I am a benefactor.

But you, my reader, you can also feel that pride of helping to lift the lives of other people.

The children we help today, are our caregivers in the future. They will not only care for us, and future generations, but for our communities, businesses, and the earth.

The philosopher Lao Tzu taught about teaching a man to fish. This is what I do. For one long weekend out of the year, I provide space for the Florida Writers Foundation's biggest fundraiser of grant money. The money is passed to helpful programs, and the next generations rise.

If you are willing to help me help them, here are your options:
- Just flat-out donate money. No auction items or bids necessary. Go to the FWF website: floridawritersfoundation.net/donate-here.
- Decide to donate a desirable auction item. Download the donation form at the same link and fill it out.

Email it to tamilowe@gmail.com and either ship her the item or bring it to the hotel at the conference.
- Attend the Annual Writers Conference and bid REPEATEDLY on your favorite items. You don't have to use the items; you can give them away as Christmas gifts.

I sincerely wish for your optimal health, enough to mask up and come see me. As a high bidder, I also am giving to you. The giving is endless, and I am amazing.

See you there,

The Dogwood Room

Hilton Orlando/Altamonte Springs

—A Characterization by Tami Lowe Whiting

Section Six

Florida Writers Foundation

Florida Writers Foundation

by Tami Lower Whiting
Florida Writers Foundation Director

If you have attended a Florida Writers Conference in Altamonte Springs, you may have seen Florida Writers Association (FWA) and Florida Writers Foundation (FWF) used in various conference materials or on signs in the hall. Even among Florida Writers Association veteran members, there has been some confusion about what FWF is and what it does. I am excited to share the purpose of FWF and spread the word about what we hope to do to affect change.

What do we do?

We are Florida Writers Foundation, Inc., a 501(c)(3) non-profit corporation. We are a sister organization to FWA. Our goal is to promote reading literacy, and also enhance the writing skills of children, youth, and adults. FWF provides grants to schools and initiatives.

We sponsored a published compilation of student-teacher writing in Pinellas County Elementary Schools. We sponsored books to Title 1 schools in Brevard

County, a 3rd grade writing contest at Belleview-Santos, and a 6th grade contest in Osceola. In the Palm Beach area, we sponsor an essay writing challenge in middle and high schools. We also sponsor an anthology at Chiles Academy in Daytona Beach, which serves an eclectic and diverse community of pregnant and parenting teens. We also sponsor "1000 Books before Kindergarten," a reading program in Mt. Dora.

Silent Auction: let's go shopping!

Florida Writers Association's members help us to raise funds every year at their conference! Our Silent Auction at FWA's conference is one of our biggest fundraisers. Held at the Hilton Orlando/Altamonte Springs, hundreds of writers, editors, and publishers gather for a weekend of writing workshops, networking opportunities, and award presentations. The Silent Auction will be a featured event, and many items are shown on FWF's website floridawritersfoundation.com and social media:

Facebook @FLoridaWritersFoundation,
Instagram @floridawritersfoundation,
Twitter @WritersFlorida

Celebrity Workshop

The Foundation sponsors an all-day workshop at the start of the FWA's Writers Conference. FWF workshops always provide essential writing advice and information to FWA member authors. Attending the workshop also helps to provide funds for FWF-sponsored programs.

Got A Grant Idea?

We encourage all who would like to apply for an FWF grant to help with literacy to do so. Got an idea? Applicants may submit a packet that includes a cover letter, the application from the FWF website, and the requested documents.

Application Process: Visit our website, floridawriters-foundatlon.com to download the appropriate application. Scholarship applications should be submitted by May 1st, and grant applications by September 1st. The Committee will review the applications and notify applicants within two months whether they have been selected. Public announcement of the scholarships and grants will be made at the Florida Writers Celebrity Workshop in the fall. Recipients will be invited to the conference, where they will be given the funds. Applicants who are not selected to receive a scholarship or grant are welcome to reapply the following year.

Reapplying the Following Year: Applicants who were not selected to receive a scholarship or grant are welcome to reapply the next year. Those who were selected to receive funds are also welcome to reapply the following year. Recipients of an award do not automatically receive funds the next time around. Each award is a one-time scholarship or grant.

Getting the Word Out: The Florida Writers Foundation wants as many organizations as possible to know about the opportunities to apply for the FWF grants. Information is disseminated electronically by email and social media. The information is also included in all our Conference materials and announcements. Plus, news releases are issued for the award announcements at the fall Florida Writers Celebrity Workshop.

Follow-up for Grant Recipients: Representatives of the organization should report back with photographs and event results of the grant-supported programs or projects.

For More Information, contact Melody Dimick, Florida Writers Foundation President: dimickmelodydean@gmail.com

Recent Testimonial:

"I volunteer for Florida Writer's Foundation (FWF.) The FWF fundraises for grant money which they award to literacy programs in our state. Access to books is a con-sistent goal for many organizations and volunteers in our communities. To get books into the homes of children on every street and part of town is a worthy goal. If you have an idea for helping in this effort, you can submit a grant proposal found at our website, floridawritersfoundation. net. These are the stats we use under our letterhead on our donation forms:

'Twenty-five percent of Florida's fourth graders do not pass the yearly reading assessment, and sixty per-cent are not at reading level. Twenty-five percent of adult Floridians read at an eighth-grade level or lower and one in eight is functionally illiterate. We invite you to join us in doing something meaningful about these statistics.'

What can we do to help? First, establish your own sphere of influence, at the core. Then add a layer when you feel good about leveling up. You'll know when you've got that core solid. I encourage all of us to reach beyond our homes, to find the one. The ripple effect is incalcu-lable. Of course, giving to others brings happiness and purpose to us as well."

—*Tami Whiting*

Section Seven

Florida Writers Association Youth

Florida Writers Association Youth

by Mark H. Newhouse
FWAY Chairperson, 1917 to present
FWA Board of Directors

A phone call started it for me. When Chris Coward asked if I was interested in taking over the Florida Writers Association youth program, my first inclination was to head for the hills. But, as a retired teacher, parent, and author of children's books, how could I turn down the opportunity to work with middle and high school students who love writing? I thought how much I would have loved having the incredible resources and support of an FWA when I was younger, and I was hooked. But what was I getting into?

A day at the annual Florida Writers Youth Conference, October 2017, hosted by Kristen Steiffel and co-chair Serena Schreiber, introduced me to eager young minds sponging up information delivered by entertaining and informative presenters. I was impressed that these aspiring writers were there to learn and network with each other. They were also there to cheer for each other during the Youth Awards Luncheon where their achievements were honored in the Royal Palm Literary Awards competition and the FWA Collection contest in front of hundreds of adult FWA members. I was blown away by their enthusiasm and excitement as winners were announced to loud applause by the supportive FWA audience. I witnessed the pride of parents and families when the finalists and winners were presented with their hard-earned awards.

Not long after that inspiring ceremony, the Collection winners became "official" authors with their book signing event. I remembered how excited I was the first time I signed a book and saw that sense of accomplishment in the faces of these new young authors autographing the Collection book for their friends and adult FWA members. How wonderful for these students to add "published author" and "RPLA Winner" to their college and career applications. FWA makes that happen and I had to be part of that.

Taking over any program can be challenging, but with the support of the FWA Board of Directors, Committee Chairs, FWAY continues to serve our middle and high school students. Covid-19 made live meetings impossible, so we shifted gears and established the 2nd Tuesday

FWAY Online Writing Club, which meets, naturally, the second Tuesday of each month, 7-9 PM. At these friendly meetings, we feature special guests, lots of tips and practical help, as well as sharing work. Hosted by our Youth Representative to the FWA Board of Directors, Michael Farrell, with FWAY Chairperson, Mark H. Newhouse, as the adult supervisor, and FWAY Co-Chair, Paula Feuerstein, as backup, we encourage youth members to suggest topics they want discussed. Recent meetings provided FWAY members tips on how to submit work for RPLA competition and the Collection contest, as well as how to "Break Writers Block," "Find Ideas," "Plan Practically Perfect Plots," and "Create Compelling Characters." Attendees experience hands-on presentations in a professional atmosphere restricted to FWAY members only. While we hope to initiate new, live, Writing Clubs soon, we will continue these invaluable monthly get-togethers with our writing friends.

Each year, our members are invited to attend the Florida Writers Youth Conference. We look for presenters who have knowledge and experience, but who can deliver exciting and interactive programs. Recent conferences have featured top presenters from FWA, thanks to Conference Coordinator, Chrissy Jackson. A highlight each year is the Q&A session with bestselling authors, renowned agents, and publishers. Held at the end of the day, these interviews with super-stars are a unique learning event that culminates in an exciting day. Attendees leave with new inspiration, knowledge, and friends. They spend the day with young people from all over Florida who share their passion and enthusiasm. Many have already said they can't wait until the next October when they'll be together again.

FWAY has a new logo, a symbol of the new directions we are exploring to begin the next decade. FWA's commitment to help all writers, including our youth members, honoring our differences, is an invaluable contribution to the future. I am grateful to be a link in the history of FWA's effort to help our children and look forward to working on the FWAY with our devoted volunteers and highly motivated youth members.

Thank you for this opportunity to share the story of FWAY. For more information and materials to start a local FWAY Writing Club in a school, library, or bookstore near you, please contact me using the form at www. newhousecreativegroup.com. Help youth writers and earn FBFLs = Best Fans for Life. We have everything you need to join the FWAY Wave. I've had a blast working with these great kids and am grateful to the Board and members of FWA for all the support of our youth.

A Youth Testimonial:

by Michael Farrell
FWA Youth Members Representative
FWA Board of Directors

My journey with the Florida Writers Association began halfway through 2019. I was trying to find my way into the writing world, so I went online and found a list of writing conferences in Florida. From the list, I ultimately chose the Florida Writers Association and attended the conference later that year. The welcoming atmosphere and informative workshops had me hooked. It gave me the opportunity to meet many kind and passionate writers. At the Royal Palm Literary Awards Banquet, I happened to sit next to an author who won a gold award, which motivated me to prepare something for both the RPLA competition and the Collection contest for the next year.

2020 rolled around and then, out of the blue, I was contacted by FWA's Board of Directors. They wanted a youth representative and chose me to fill the role. After some further communication, I received a warm welcome onto the board.

Once on the board, I became devoted to FWAY, the Florida Writers Association's youth program filled with talented, aspiring young writers. I joined the FWAY team with other members whom I had first met at the conference in 2019. I now host a monthly writing club, as well as manage the FWAY Instagram page.

Besides FWAY, I have gotten the chance to chair a committee for the board and interview many of our authors, one of whom is the RPLA gold award winning author that I sat next to at the 2019 conference.

I pursued writing as a way to express my creativity and found a place where I can meet and work with other creative people. I chose FWA, and FWA chose me. I'm excited to see what the future holds, for both my writing career and the Florida Writers Association.

Section Eight

Florida Writers Book Expo

Florida Writers Book Expo

Arielle Haughee
Florida Writers Book Expo Chair

In May 2021, FWA sponsored its first Book Expo. Because of the pandemic, this Book Expo was done remotely. The Expo was an online multi-day event where partic- ipating authors and publishers purchased a "booth" to sell their books. Genres included: Children, Romance, Science Fiction and Fantasy, Thriller, Suspense, and Action Adventure. Mystery and Horror, Historical Fiction, General Fiction, Nonfiction, Memoir, and Poetry. Genres were open to adjustment to adapt to the number of booths. For example, if a large amount of Horror reservations came in, we made Horror its own category.

The event was marketed to readers of all genres. Incentives were provided for visiting and making pur- chases. Publishers had the opportunity to decide on the best location for their booth based on their authors and books. Publishers also had the option to purchase a second booth in a different genre category location.

In all, sixty FWA authors participated. Participating authors and publishers marketed the event using their normal marketing streams. This included newslet- ters, social media, word-of-mouth, and any other mar- keting method normally used. Graphics were provided for sharing purposes. FWA also marketed the event to readers.

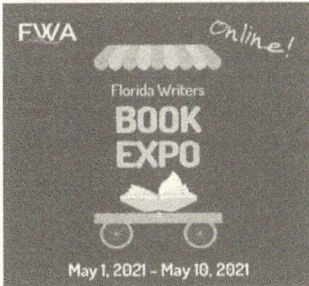

The authors and publishers received their booths, an event t-shirt, and access to an exclusive advanced marketing class with CEO of Author Marketing Expert Penny Sansevieri, CEO and founder of Author Marketing Experts, Inc. (AME). Penny is an Adjunct Professor at NYU, a best-selling author, and internationally recognized book marketing and media relations expert. Her company is one of the leaders in the publishing industry and has developed some of the most cutting-edge book marketing campaigns. Her advanced marketing class focused on current book selling trends, what works and what doesn't. Authors were also entered in a drawing for a free 2022 RPLA entry.

By a measure, the Expo was a success. The expo site had over 6,300 views. A majority of the participants noted an increase, if not in sales of their books, then in visibility and exposure.

Section Nine

Writers Groups

Writers Groups

Amelia Island Writers

by *Marla McDaniel*
Amelia Island Writers Group Leader

The Amelia Island Writers (Bay County) meets on the fourth Tuesday of every month. Speakers, critiques, discussions, and readings are featured at the meetings. Marla McDaniel is the Group Leader.

Amelia Island Writers (A/W) continues to grow its programs and numbers of participants. A/W is the Nassau County chapter of Florida Writers Association, a 501©6 nonprofit organization unified under the banner of "Writers Helping Writers."

The chapter had its beginnings in the mid-eighties while Lucy Beebe Tobias, chapter founder, was a reporter with the News Leader (newspaper). Lucy, a published author, eventually relocated to Sarasota. Her monthly Saturday Morning Magazine about Florida culture and travel is a popular blog throughout the state and beyond.

The chapter was then assumed by group leader Maggie DeVries, owner of Books Plus. *Ghosts of Amelia and Other Tales*, and *Amelia Island's Golden Years, Silver Tears* continue to be popular with residents and visitors alike. News Leader columnist Cara Curtin and cohorts wrote a few novels together, beginning in 2004 with *Murder in Fernandina.* Change is inevitable, and a decade ended when Maggie and her husband returned to Charleston after closing that bookstore.

The chapter almost folded at that point. Dr. Nadine Vaughan D'Ardenne, her husband, Dave D'Ardenne, Marla McDaniel, Jim Weinsier, and several others were determined to keep it going. Writers by the Sea was born. After five years as group leader, Nadine retired to spend more time with her own writing. She is a screenwriter and published author.

Amelia Island Writers re-emerged from Writers by the Sea in 2019 with Marla McDaniel as group leader. A comprehensive website was established along with a monthly newsletter to bring the writing community together and celebrate the accomplishments of local writers. An active advisory committee plans author chats, programs, and workshops. Katherine Hoehn, Pat Martocci, Lee Ann Shobe, Michael Stokes, and Jim Weinsier coordinate various facets of the local group. Micah Ward, an integral part of A/W, has moved to Tennessee, but is an occasional visitor back to the island. Dr. Diane LaRochelle, A/W coordinator of interactive programs, passed away in 2020.

Listing local authors past and present on the AW website is a recent project. Serving to showcase our creative community, this public resource provides a convenient way to locate area authors and their books. Bloggers and businesses in support of writers are also included.

Programs include several focus groups with a possibility of more to come. Included are Critique, Writing for Stage and Screen Writing, Memoirs or Biographies. Works in Progress, and Amelia Island Authors with a focus on collaborative writing and working with local artists. A/W is pleased to be part of the northeast Florida chapters, with Vic DiGenti as Regional Director.

Delray Beach Open Readings

Barbara Cronie
Delray Beach Writers' Colony Director

Open Read Night at Delray Beach. Delray Beach's Writers' Colony Director, Barbara Cronie, spent years in New York City's Greenwich Village and Gramercy Park rubbing elbows with writers, poets, and other writerly souls. Remarkably touched by her experience reading her poetry at open reading sessions at St. Mark's Church in the Bowery, Barbara introduced the concept at Old School Square Creative Arts School.

The Writers' Colony joined the Creative Arts School at Old School Square in 2009, offering writing courses, critique groups, workshops, and publishing seminars. In 2014, Open Readings evolved as an outreach program in the community, free of charge, to residents and visitors. Once a month, published and unpublished writers, poets and curious listeners gather for two hours, offering sup-port and motivation.

Open Readings is different from most writing groups in that we don't critique. Our sole purpose is to encourage writers, wherever they are in their journey. We offer the opportunity to be heard and an audience that listens. Our partici-pants cross all demographic lines, levels of experience, and writing genres. We've had everything from Jewish haikus to prison memoirs, to a main character getting kicked in the head by a cow. And then there's Gloria—whose hilarious essays on dating in her senior years causes many to blush.

Readers, like author Hartley Barnes and writer Tajuana Troy, in picture at right, take their place at the lectern in a room of several round tables for eight. Typically, fifteen or so attendees listen with a cup of coffee and cookie or two, with friends, old and new. Depending on attendance, readers are allotted ten minutes—more if time allows. It's the reader's choice whether or not to take questions about the content of their piece.

We're a laid-back, informal group with a no-stress philosophy. Many writers just listen for a session or more before they feel comfortable enough to read their original work. The gleam in a writer's eye when they're done reading is a boost to everyone in the room. We have but one rule—respect for one another. Appreciation and applause come naturally.

Former FWA Vice President and current Board Member Herb Sennett, was spot on when he said during his visit to our Open Readings, "You have something very special here." Indeed, we do.

Ponte Vedra Writing Group

by Vic DiGenti
Group Leader and FWA Regional Director

The Ponte Vedra Writers Group meets on the fourth Saturday of every month. Speakers, as well as critiques, discussions, and readings, are featured at the meetings. Vic DiGenti is the Group Leader.

I became an FWA member in the first year or two after the organization was launched. I recall attending a few of founding member Glenda Ivey's talks before and after she started FWA 20 years ago and writers groups were scarce and far between. Eventually, the Beaches Palm Group (Palm Group was the initial designation given to the writers groups) appeared at the Ponte Vedra Beach Library, close to where I live. I attended that group for a year or so when the group leader abdicated. Rather than see the group dissolve, I volunteered to lead the group and my first meeting (as I recall) was in January of 2005.

Following the lead of the previous leader and other groups, we met monthly and presented featured speakers. I drew from the bank of local authors, editors, and creative writing professors. Steven K. Brown, a local private investigator and author of *The Complete Idiot's Guide to Private Investigating*, was one of my first speakers. Other speakers the first few years included Bill Kerr, author of the *Matt Berkely Adventure* series, children's and YA writer June Weitman, editor and book coach Lyn Harlin, Flagler College creative writing professor Dr. Darien Andreu, attorney Carolyn Herman advising writers on publishing contracts, and SF author Sandra McDonald.

Our group continued to grow, averaging about thirty writers per meeting, and in 2006 FWA did away with the Palm Group designation, and we became the Ponte Vedra Writers Group. Somewhere in either 2006 or 2007, I joined the FWA Board and was named a Regional Director of NE Florida. We already had writers groups in Ponte Vedra Beach and Jacksonville and I worked to expand our brand throughout NE Florida. Over the next few years, we added a group in St. Augustine (St. Johns County) with Randy Cribbs as the first group leader there. In Nassau County, Judy Connolly was one of the first leaders of the Jacksonville Central WG, and Jim Morgan the first of the Fernandina Beach WG. Later, in 2010 I would recruit Maureen Jung to lead the Clay County Writers Group, which she did effectively until last year. Although there have been, and continue to be, changes in the leadership of these five groups, they are all still in existence.

In 2007, working with other writers from Ponte Vedra WG, we jumped off the deep end and produced the first of our one-day mini-conferences along with a regional book awards competition modeled after the RPLA competition. We called ours the Lighthouse Book Awards. The May 19, 2007, conference titled "Shift Your Writing into High

Gear," with a race car logo, was keynoted by international best-selling author Steve Berry. We offered a number of concurrent sessions and announced the Lighthouse Book Award finalists at lunch. The event was a smashing success and we repeated it in 2008, this one titled "Swing for the Stars—Be the Best Writer YOU Can Be." We had two keynoters at this conference, Philip F. Deaver and Jack McDevitt, plus eight workshops and announced the 2008 Lighthouse Book Awards winners.

Whew! Those events were a lot of work, and we exhausted our corps of volunteers, so they were the last of our extracurricular activities as far as the one-day conferences and awards competitions. But we plugged away, representing FWA at regional book festivals like the Amelia Island Book Festival, Jacksonville's Much Ado About Books, and St. Augustine's Florida Heritage Book Festival, where we had tables and signed up interested writers for FWA.

In 2009, I partnered with local author and screenwriter Sharon Cobb, working with the University of North Florida, to launch the UNF Writers Conference. This was a three-day event and attracted well over 100 writers. Because of my commitment to the conference and association with FWA, UNF agreed to list FWA as one of the sponsors. It was at the 2010 conference that I met and recruited Maureen Jung to lead the Clay County WG. We continued the conference in 2011, and although we enjoyed another large turnout, the university decided it was costing them too much money and suspended the event after that. One of the innovations I brought to the UNF Writers Conference was the Saturday morning block of critique workshops. I recruited three or four well-respected writers to lead these popular workshops.

I had joined the fledgling Florida Heritage Book Festival as Co-Director in 2008 and helped them expand the event with a day of writers workshops.

What else? The Ponte Vedra WG has proven successful over the years, attracting anywhere from fifteen to sixty writers at each meeting, with the numbers dependent on who the speaker might be. Panel discussions proved to be one of our more popular presentations. Over the years we've presented author panels covering many genres and topics, including indie publishing, romance writing, mystery and thriller writing, memoirs, and children's books.

And in this past challenging year, where our library meeting rooms have been closed, I've tried to keep the fires burning by offering Zoom webinars. This allowed us to feature more authors from throughout the state that may not have been able to attend for in-person meetings.

Suncoast Writers Guild, Inc.

Gloria Arthur
Writers Group Leader

Suncoast Writers Guild, Inc. (SWG), based in Englewood, celebrated its 30th anniversary in 2020. Our group provides a welcoming and fun haven for writers and poets to gain confidence and hone their craft. We are an eclectic mix of beginning, intermediate and seasoned writers representing many genres – authors, poets, essayists, journalists, and others – from a variety of professional backgrounds. The one thing we have in common is the understanding of just how much courage it takes for new members to leave the solitary comfort of their writing space, walk into a room of strangers, and lay bare their writing for all to see.

New members are welcome to simply listen and observe until they feel comfortable enough to share their work. Our members are always respectful and happy to offer constructive advice. In this environment of like-minded creative people, members gain confidence and improve their skills. Many have gone on to be published, nominated for prestigious awards, and won contests.

SWG was founded in 1990 with six members and four basic principles, which are just as valid today as they were then:

1. To bring together, in a professional setting, persons interested in the art of writing.
2. To exchange ideas.
3. To provide a support system.
4. To provide critiques and educational opportunities.

The membership quickly grew to nearly fifty. SWG published its first *Inklings* anthology and hosted a two-day conference with attendees from all over Florida.

The Guild's regular business meeting, which includes a guest speaker, is held on the first Saturday of the month (on hiatus June-September). The Guild offers three additional monthly meetings, Poetry Pod, Long Writers, and a Readers Workshop.

Opportunities for our members to showcase their talents:

- *Inklings* anthology. This regular publication includes members' poems and prose.
- PenPoints newsletter. Our monthly newsletter includes members' works as well as a business updates, notices of upcoming programs and tips to improve writing skills.
- Facebook. Members can post announcements of their new publications, awards, and other news on the SWG Facebook page, and periodically member websites are highlighted. https://www.facebook.com/suncoastwriters/
- SWG website. Members can promote their published books on our website and link to their own author websites:
- http://www.suncoastwriters.com/. Our site is also linked to the Florida Writers Association.
- The Little Band of Writers. Formed in 2007, the group combines musical talent with writing talent. Members write their own lyrics, and the group has performed at restaurants, nursing homes and other venues. Although not currently performing in public, they still do jam sessions for our annual luncheons.

Community Involvement. One of the Guild's biggest strengths is our firm commitment to community involvement.

- The Hermitage Artist Retreat: One of our members is the designated liaison between SWG and this organization, which hosts writers, musicians, and authors.
- Englewood Art Center: Artists create works of art for this annual event. Poets, including SWG members, compose a poem which is posted beside the art.
- School poetry contests: SWG contributes to and participates in the Englewood Elementary School

contest and the Lemon Bay High School Poetry Shout Out at the Bay contest.

- Venice Book Fair: SWG hosts a table at this annual event, where visitors can learn more about SWG and members have an opportunity to see their books.
- Island Walk: Art in the Afternoon: Artists create works of art for this annual event. Writers, including SWG members, compose a story about one of the works and present it before a live audience.
- Local author book displays. Our members are afforded an opportunity to promote their books through displays in local libraries.
- Local fairs and festivals. Over the years, SWG has participated in several fairs and festivals in a variety of ways. The Little Band of Writers have performed, some members have written and produced plays, while others have written clue books for a scavenger hunt.
- Local author bookshelf at Elsie Quirk Library in Englewood. Patrons can discover and borrow our members books.

- Denny Girard Youth Writing Contest. In conjunction with the Elsie Quirk Library, SWG is currently developing this contest.

We will continue to seek out additional opportunities to learn, grow and give back to our community while maintaining our four founding principles, which encourage members to develop their own skills and support other writers. Please visit either our Facebook page, or our website for more info. https://www.facebook.com/suncoastwriters/, http://www.suncoastwriters.com/.

2013 Indie Publishing panel. Left to right: Vic DiGenti, Sharon Cobb, Rik Feeney, Cheyenne Knopf, and Judith White.

2014 Children's Book panel. Left to right: Jane Wood, Jules Coffey Santella, Jennifer Swanson, and June Wellman.

Freedom Writers Group

Carol Jones
Writers Group Leader

The Freedom Writers Group meets on the last Thursday of every month. Speakers, as well as critiques, discussions, and readings, are featured at the meetings. Carol Jones is the Group Leader.

The Freedom Writers Group, Ocala, has existed since 2005 when Lyn Hill registered the group with FWA. The current membership totals thirty-two. Meeting attendance is anywhere from ten to twenty-two, depending on the agenda and time of year. When the COVID-19 coronavirus pandemic of 2020 shut down our physical meetings in March, the group went online to continue story exchanges and critiques.

Ocala's Good Life (OGL) magazine editor, Dean Blinkhorn, selected seven stories from our group for their Nov/Dec 2020 Holiday Memories issue. In 2017, the Freedom Writers published *Hey, Got a Minute?* a collection of eighty-seven short stories by twenty-six authors. OGL favored us with a six-page book review in their May/June issue. In 2013, our *Favorite Vacation Tales* appeared in OGL's Jul/Aug issue, and in November 2011, they printed nine of our Thanksgiving and Christmas stories. We have been invited to submit stories again later in 2021.

Sponsored by the Friends of Freedom Public Library during their month-long Terrific Tuesday's event, the writers group presented Meet the Authors Day on November 15, 2011.

A few members enjoyed participating in author expos and radio interviews, and we presented another Authors Day on December 19, 2018.

At the invitation of the Friends, we displayed our published books at their annual meeting on January 25, 2020.

Royal Palm Literary Awards Winners:

2020 – Angie Mayo, second-place award for her Creative Nonfiction, *Natasha's Garden*. Angie serves as an RPLA judge.

2019 – Lynn Bechdolt, third-place award in the General Catch-All unpublished category for *The Price of Admission*. Lynn also serves as an RPLA judge.

2016 – Beverly Johnson Biehr won first place for her memoir, *Casualties of Peacemaking*. Beverly currently gives presentations and book signings.

2013 – R.M. Prioleau won first place under Published Novella for *The Necromancer's Apprentice*. Rebecca has published eight books to date and has another nearly finished.

2011 – Carol Jones won first place for her Unpublished Science Fiction novel, *Broken Diamond*. Carol served for several years as an RPLA judge.

FWA Collections:

C.C. Gallo and Carol Jones both have stories published in various FWA Collection volumes.

The Florida Writer:

Angie Mayo, Lynn Bechdolt and Carol Jones have published in *The Florida Writer* and other magazines. Carol Jones published an article in Marion County Library System's magazine, *WORDS*.

Trilogies:

Robin Collison contributed to *Forgiveness is the Hardest Thing: How 20 Women Let Go*, to be published in November 2021, and finished two trilogies, *The Listener of Morpho Island*, winner of three pre-publication first prizes, and *The Fine Art Club of Shrimpboat Key*, winner of one pre-publication prize.

Novels:

Rachel Thompson published four novels and one sci-fi anthology and has two books in progress.

Terry Tibbetts published *A Spartan Game* in 2012.

Ten Pizza published *Healthy Eating Recipes* in 2015 and 2016, and her novelized memoir, *DNA: Do Not Assume* in 2020.

Poetry:

Lynn Bechdolt, Beverly Gilewitz and Angie Mayo won and placed in various poetry contests, resulting in publication of their work.

Drama:

Judy Gill, drama writer and playwright, wrote and presented two plays at the On Top of the World theater, and a third play written by James J. Jenkins. Four of our authors held roles in the plays, sporting their acting as well as writing abilities.

Memoirs:

Jim Whitehead is putting the final touches on his memoir, *One Body—Two Lives.*

Carol Jones is finishing her duo-memoir with her sister, *A Tale of Two Sisters.*

Anthony LaPenta, author of *The Sniper*, is compiling his flash fiction into a memoir.

Rica Keenum published her memoir of motherhood, *Petals of Rain.*

Columnists:

Mary Ellen Saladino has been published in *The Florida Gardening* magazine and has been a contributing writer and columnist for Ocala's *Good Life* magazine since 2011. She celebrates her 10th anniversary with OGL this year.

Erin Baliya writes for the *South Marion Citizen* and *West Marion Messenger* weekly newspapers. Her fiction appears on Amazon.com under the pen name Drew Stephens.

Ed Centanni, computer software writer and author of several published short stories, publishes the newsletter *Flight Feathers* for the One Wing Low Squadron (OWLS) RC Club.

Technical Writers:

Beverly Gilewitz writes in the technical genre as do Rachel Thompson and Karen Lowry. Karen served on our

HEY book committee in 2011 along with Anthony LaPenta, Lyn Hill, R.M. Prioleau and Carol Jones.

The Freedom Writers Group, Ocala

Angie Mayo, Anthony LaPenta, Jr., Beverly Biehr, Beverly Gilewitz, Brenda Elliott, Carol Jones, Carrie Schachter, C.C. Gallo, Cindy Pontbriand, Diane Bannard, Ed Centanni, Erin Baliya, Frank Dole, Gail Corley, James J. Jenkins, Jim Whitehead, John Zanyk, Judy Gill, Karen Lowry, Lair Glaudell, Lyn Hill, Lynn Bechdolt, Mary Ellen Saladino, Rachel Thompson, Rebecca (R.M.) Prioleau, Rica Keenum, Robin Collison, Teri Pizza, Terry Tibbetts

Together our group continues to write and critique each other's short stories, memoirs, and novels, bound by one goal: to encourage each member toward a higher level of writing. In the process, we learn and improve, a project that's never finished.

Volusia County Writing Groups

Veronica H. Hart
Writers Group Leader and Regional Director

Volusia County members of the Florida Writers Association are a prolific and talented group. So many writers have come and gone over the past twenty years, I can only say that they all helped the organization grow into a well-respected enterprise. After reaching out to the current writing group leader, I am posting many of the members' comments and accomplishments. Flagler and Putnam counties do not have official FWA writing groups at this time.

"A Quiet Place in the Country," Julie Eberhart Painter told me when I asked about a local writers group back in 2005. "We meet at my house, but Marcia Ford is the Writing Group Leader." I had visions of a cemetery, but the housing estate was exactly as described, far out of town in a quiet place in the country.

I had joined the Florida Writers Association in January of 2002 while still living in New York State. We had a home in Daytona Beach, but I only came down for about six weeks in the winter. I let a year lapse, then rejoined in 2004 and went to my first meeting at Julie's in 2005 by which time we, my husband and I, had moved here permanently. For me, it was coming home to Florida, for Bob it was another new adventure in living.

Since then, with the support of writing groups, I have published, both traditionally and self, thirteen books, including five in a series called *The Blenders* through Champagne Books, a 2009 first place winner in the RPLA. My stories also appear in several of the FWA Collection volumes.

The first group in Volusia County included Julie, Darlene Duncan, Marcia Ford, Mike Pyle, me and two or three others. These particular members have since become traditionally and/or self-published authors, some both.

Since those first beginnings, Volusia County evolved to have five writing groups, Port Orange Scribes—Part I and Part II, Daytona Area Fiction Writers, Daytona Writers, and the group that meets in Deland, and I evolved to become the Regional Director for Volusia, Flagler, and Putnam counties. The Flagler County dissolved about five years ago when both group leaders moved to other states. Members from there now attend Daytona meetings.

One of the best ways to help explain why the FWA has grown and works so well is to listen to what the members have to say.

William G. Collins: "I was happy to join the Daytona Writers Group in 2015 with my first ancient Egyptian novel *Behind the Golden Mask*. That same year I joined the Port Orange Scribes and published *A Leper's Tale*. Both books were published that same year, 2015. They are both novels, fiction, historical genre. I could not have published on my own, really. I needed the excellent input from other members of the group. Their comments and suggestions were invaluable, as they are today. I joined FWA that same year and have received, through workshops and annual conferences, invaluable help in becoming a better writer. Friendships made through FWA have contributed to my growth as an author." (Note: Bill has gone on to publish at least twenty-seven more books. He is the Port Orange Scribes Facilitator. He is also represented in FWA Collection volumes.)

Marie Brack joined in 2014 and published her first nonfiction, *A Writer's Sampler*, in 2015 and then her first fiction in 2016. *A Writer's Sampler* was an award winner in an RPLA competition.

Walter Doherty joined in 2008 and had his first fiction published in the 2013 FWA Collection, *It's A Crime!*

Chris Holmes joined Daytona Writers in 2009. Her published work includes *Inky*, a novella, *Light a Candle*, *Chase the Devil Away*, and *Vamped: The Turning*. Both won gold medals (2019 and 2020) in the RPLA annual writing competition. Her writing has also appeared in several Collection volumes.

Robin Mimna: "Most people don't understand how important my writing group has been for me. Daytona Area Writers not only improved my writing (and there was much room for improvement) but helped me cope during a difficult time in my life. The support and encouragement I received uncovered a path I didn't realize I was searching for. I went back to school, finished my book, and started another. The only thing better than being the recipient of such support is providing it to my group members in return. Our group has been in operation for over thirty years, and I intend to make sure it stays that way for another thirty." (Note: Robin refers to the fact that Daytona Area Fiction Writers began as an independent group somewhere in the late 80s and eventually changed over to an FWA group around 2010.)

Her book, *Hating Jesse Harmon* won a gold medal as well as Unpublished Book of the Year in 2019.

Bob Hart: "I joined the FWA in 2005. I'm told we went to an early conference in the Tampa area with Ronnie prior to my becoming a member, but that one I don't remember. The first conference I remember was at Disney World where I worked as a volunteer on the registration desk. There was one computer and only one person knew how to use it. Long lines formed. I took over the complaints line which never lacked for upset attendees.

I stayed a volunteer at all subsequent conferences, for many years working in the bookstore with A.J. Robinson, Jo Ann, and their daughter Alexa.

My main take away from all those years was the value of FWA sponsored critique groups. In this, I was helped by being a member of Toastmasters. I found I learned as much reading and critiquing others, as I did from attempting my own writing. Much of the value lay in the internet answers to the questions that arose when trying to critique.

I maintained my FWA writing presence by submitting ten articles, usually humorous, to the FWA magazine and writing many more which were not submitted, and to the annual collections contest which started in 2009. My work has appeared in all but one of the Collections." (Note: He has published: *Twisted Knickers*, *Cage Liners*, *Petpourii*, *Spears and Promises*, and *Oliver's Rubaiyat*. He also won RPLA awards for his short stories over the years.)

Laura Andrews: "I joined City Island Fiction Writers in spring, 2007. Started judging for FWA-RPLA in 2009 following a recommendation by Ronnie Hart. I then joined the FWA in 2010. My first short story sale (*The Legend of Johnny Bell*/Laura Andrews) was in 2013. Got my agent for novels in 2017. Published first novel with Blue Breech Press in 2020 (*Ghost*/Elle Andrews Patt)."

Current members of the Port Orange Scribes, besides Bill Collins, who have published books are:

Mary Kay Pyles – *Rise and Shine Rosie.*

Joan Harris – *A Princess, A Prince, and a Dragon; A Princess, A Prince and a Dragon Go to a Camp; The Royal Dragon Goes to School.*

Joyce Senatro – *First Class to America; The Middle of Somewhere.*

Rebekah Mead – *What's Eating You?* (She self-published then pulled it back for much-needed edits).

Diane Boilard is published in numerous FWA Collection volumes as well as in a collection of Canadian stories. Her "paragraphs" have also been in several issues of *The Florida Writer* magazine.

Seminole County Writers Group

Joan Levy
Writers Group Leader

The Seminole Writers Group meets at the Bay County Library on the first Tuesday of every month. Speakers, as well as critiques, discussions, and readings, are featured at the meetings. Joan Levy is the Group Leader.

Florida Writers Conference, two empty seats, three determined writers, and perhaps a touch of serendipity? It happened at the 2009 Royal Palm Literary Awards Banquet.

Two empty seats remained at a banquet table near the back of the crowded ballroom. The woman didn't know anyone at the table when she asked to sit there. With few seats remaining before the RPLA dinner, another woman approached and asked woman #1 if she could sit in the remaining seat.

Their personalities clicked, and they talked about writing throughout the banquet. At the conference the next day, they met during breaks and lunch. At one of the breaks, woman #1 ran into a man she had known from an organization they belonged to. Seems he had started writing novels and short stories. She introduced woman #2 and the man.

Their conversation turned to writers groups—what they liked and didn't like. Each of them expressed a need to find a good writers group. Their needs were the same—a short story critique group with a strong foundation and serious writer-members.

Each of them wished for that type of writers group. But as wish-laden conversations go—sometimes they don't. However, this one took off.

The trio met many times over the next year to hammer out details. Build it and they will come became their mantra. With a plan in place, they ran an ad in the newspaper and arranged for a meeting room at the Lake Mary Library.

On March 24, 2011, the threesome arranged tables and chairs in the library meeting room. They laughed at the possibility that writers may not show up and they'd be the only ones in the group. When the doors opened that evening, five writers walked in. The Seminole County Writers Group (SCW) was born.

Original members and others who've joined since that night a decade ago have contributed to the strength of SCW. Each writer is dedicated to helping member works improve. They've won many RPLA awards and have published books and short stories.

There hasn't been a year when member stories haven't won awards at RPLA or have been published in the Collection volumes. In the latest FWA Collection, volume thirteen, *Footprints*, seven member-stories were among the sixty highest scoring winning submissions allowed in the book. And three of them won honors among the Person of Renown's Top Ten Favorites. Yowza!

Bottom line, there would be no Seminole County Writers group if it weren't for FWA, two empty seats, three determined writers, and that touch of serendipity.

Panama City Writers Group

Michael Brim
Writers Group Leader

The Panama City Writers Group meets at the Bay County Library on the last Thursday of every month. Speakers, as well as critiques, discussions, and readings, are featured at the meetings. Michael Brim is the Group Leader.

Next Door Writers Critique Group

Laurance Davis
Writers Group Leader

The Next-Door Writers Critique Group (Brevard County) meets at the Palm Bay County Public Library on the last Thursday of every month. Critiques, discussions, and readings are featured at the meetings. Laurance Davis is the Group Leader.

Space Coast Fiction Writers

Linda Wright
Writers Group Leader

The Space Coast Fiction Writers Group meets at the Suntree Viera Library the fourth Wednesday of every month. Speakers, as well as critiques, discussions, and readings, are featured at the meetings. Linda Wright is the Group Leader.

Clay County Writers Group

Paula Hilton
Writers Group Leader

The Clay County Writers Group meets at the Orange Park Public Library the third Wednesday of every month. Speakers are featured at the meetings. Paula Hilton is the Group Leader.

Marco Island Writer, Inc.

Joanne Tailele
Writers Group Leader

The Marco Island Writers Group (Collier County) meets at the Mackle Park Community Center on the second Wednesday of every month. Speakers, as well as critiques, discussions, and readings are featured at the meetings. Joanne Tailele is the Group Leader. Joanne notes, "Our local writers group on Marco Island is so pleased to have the benefits of also belonging to the Florida Writers Association. I personally get a lot of great inspirations from Florida Writers.

First Coast Christian Writers Group

Lynn Rix
Writers Group Leader

The First Coast Christian Writers Group (Duval County) meets at the Maranatha Church on the third Thursday of every month. Speakers, as well as critiques, discussions, and readings, are featured at the meetings. Lynn Rix is the Group Leader.

River City Writers

Linda Feist
Writers Group Leader

The River City Writers Group (Charlotte County) meets on the second Thursday of every month. Speakers, as well as critiques, discussions, and readings, are featured at the meetings. Linda Feist is the Group Leader.

Townie Critics Writers Group

Krys Fenner
Writers Group Leader

The Townie Critics Group (Duval County) meets on the third Sunday of every month. Critiques, discussions, and readings are featured at the meetings. Krys Fenner is the Group Leader.

Havana Writers Group

Laura Cogdill
Writers Group Leader

The Havana Writers Group (Gadsden County) meets at the Hazel Baker Community Center on the fourth Monday of every month. Critiques, discussions, and readings are featured at the meetings. Laura Cogdill is the Group Leader.

Avon Park Wordsmiths

Suzanna Crean
Writers Group Leader

The Avon Park Wordsmiths (Highland County) meets at the Avon Park Library on the first Friday every other month. Critiques, discussions, and readings are featured at the meetings. Suzanna Crean is the Group Leader.

Brandon Writers Critique Group

Carey Winters
Writers Group Leader

The Critique Group (Hillsborough County) meets on the first and third Thursday every other month. Critiques, discussions, and readings are featured at the meetings. Carey Winters is the Group Leader.

Carrollwood Writers Group

Carey Winters
Writers Group Leader

The Carrollwood Writers Group (Hillsborough County) meets at the Carrollwood Barnes and Noble on the first and third Thursday every other month. Critiques, discussions, readings, and marketing strategies are featured at the meetings. Carey Winters is the Group Leader.

Tarpon Springs Fiction Writers

David C. Edmonds
Writers Group Leader

Tarpon Springs Fiction Writers Group (Hillsborough County) meets at the Tarpon Springs Library on the first and third Thursday every other month. Critiques, discussions, and readings are featured at the meetings. David C. Edmonds is the Group Leader.

The Sounding Board

Susan Breakiron-Lowe
Writers Group Leader

The Sounding Board Writers Group (Hillsborough County) meets at the Jimmie B. Keel Regional Library on the first and third Wednesday every other month. Critiques, discussions, and readings are featured at the meetings. Susan Breakiron-Lowe is the Group Leader.

Writers Windowpane

Janet Sierzant
Writers Group Leader

The Writers Windowpane Group (Indian River County) meets at the Vero Beach Main Library every Friday. Critiques, discussions, and readings are featured at the meetings. Janet Sierzant is the Group Leader.

Lady Lake Writers Group

Christopher Malinger
Writers Group Leader

The Lady Lake Writers Group (Lake County) meets at the Lady Lake Public Library on the second and fourth Thursday of every other month. Critiques, discussions, and readings are featured at the meetings. Christopher Malinger is the Group Leader.

Tallahassee Writers Association

Pat Stanford
Writers Group Leader

The Tallahassee Writers Association (Leon County) meets at the Marzuk Shriners Temple on the second Thursday of every other month. Speakers, critiques, discussions, and readings are featured at the meetings. Pat Stanford is the Group Leader.

Yankeetown Critique Group

Lynn Sholes
Writers Group Leader

The Yankeetown Critique Group (Levy County) meets at the Inglis and Yankeetown Woman's Club every Tuesday. Critiques, discussions, and readings are featured at the meetings. Lynn Sholes is the Group Leader.

Bradenton Writers Group

David Pearce
Writers Group Leader

The Bradenton Writers Group (Manatee County) meets at Village Voices the first and third Thursday of every month. Critiques, discussions, and readings are featured at the meetings. David Pearce is the Group Leader.

Emerald Coast Writers

Jim Faris
Writers Group Leader

The Emerald Coast Writers (Okaloosa County) meets at Village Voices the second and fourth Wednesday of every month. Critiques, discussions, and readings are featured at the meetings. Jim Faris is the Group Leader.

Maitland Writers Group

Ken Pelham
Writers Group Leader

The Maitland Writers Group (Orange County) meets at the Maitland Public Library on the second Thursday of every month. Critiques, discussions, and readings are featured at the meetings. Ken Pelham is the Group Leader.

Orlando Area Writers Group

Rik Feeney
Writers Group Leader

The Orlando Area Writers Group meets at the University Club of Winter Park on the first Wednesday of every month. Speakers, critiques, discussions, and readings are featured at the meetings. Rik Feeney is the Group Leader.

East Pasco Writers Forum

Marjorie K. Nanian
Writers Group Leader

The East Pasco Writers Forum (Pasco County) meets at the Country-Aire Manor Clubhouse on the second

Thursday of every month. Critiques, discussions, and readings are featured at the meetings. Marjorie K. Nanian is the Group Leader.

Hometown Writer of Dunedin

Dick Powell
Writers Group Leader

The Hometown Writers of Dunedin (Pinellas County) meets at the Dunedin Public Library. Critiques, discussions, and readings are featured at the meetings. Dick Powell is the Group Leader.

St. Petersburg Writers Group

Maria Fox
Writers Group Leader

The St. Petersburg Writers Group meets at the St. Petersburg Public Library on the second Thursday of every month. Critiques, discussions, and readings are featured at the meetings. Maria Fox is the Group Leader.

Tampa Bay Veterans Writers Group

Maria Fox
Writers Group Leader

The Tampa Bay Veterans Writers Group is open to Military veterans, active-duty service members, spouses, and caregivers. Speakers, critiques, discussions, and readings are featured at the meetings. Maria Fox is the Group Leader.

Lakeland Writers Group

Barbara Meyers
Writers Group Leader

The Lakeland Writers Group meets at the Prime Meridian Bank on the second Wednesday of every month. Speakers, critiques, discussions, and readings are featured at the meetings. Barbara Meyers is the Group Leader.

Sarasota Writers Group

Ernie Ovitz
Writers Group Leader

The Sarasota Writers Group meets at the Nokomis Volunteer Fire Department on the first and third Wednesday of every month. Critiques, discussions, and readings are featured at the meetings. Ernie Ovitz is the Group Leader.

Seminole County Writers: A Short Story
Critique Group

Joan Levy and Beda Kantarjian
Writers Group Leaders

The Seminole County Writers: A Short Story Critique Group meets at the Oakmonte Village Lake Mary on the first and third Wednesday of every month. Critiques, discussions, and readings are featured at the meetings. Joan Levy and Beda Kantarjian are the Group Leaders.

A Novel Group of Writers

Mark McWaters and John Hope
Writers Group Leaders

A Novel Group of Writers (Seminole County) meets at the Cork & Olive on the fourth Monday of every month. Critiques, discussions, and readings are featured at the meetings. Mark McWaters and John Hope are the Group Leaders.

Ancient City Writers Group

Judy Weber
Writers Group Leader

The Ancient City Writers Group (St. Johns County) meets at the St. Johns County Public Library on the third Saturday of every month. Speakers, critiques, discussions, and readings are featured at the meetings. Judy Weber is the Group Leader.

Treasure Coast Writers Group

R. Todd Henrichs
Writers Group Leader

The Treasure Coast Writers Group (St. Lucie County) meets at the Port St. Lucie Police Department on the first and third Thursday of every month. Speakers, critiques, discussions, and readings are featured at the meetings. R. Todd Henrichs is the Group Leader.

The Treasure Coast Writers Group has seen a myriad of changes over the last few years with a change in group leaders, members publishing their works, along with the ebb and flow of members moving away and new members joining. COVID-19 presented us with issues when we couldn't meet, but the group persisted by changing to an online meeting format where we continue to critique each other's work and create an accountability in honing our craft as writers. One of our members was even recently featured in the FWA Collection, *Footprints*, an accomplishment we are all very proud of.

Oxford Writers Group

Chris Coward
Writers Group Leader

The Oxford Writers Group (Sumter County) meets at the Oxford Community Building on the first Wednesday and third Thursday of every month. Critiques and workshops are featured at the meetings. Chris Coward is the Group Leader.

Writers League of the Villages

FWA Writers Group Affiliate

The Writers League of the Villages (Sumter County) meets at the Laurel Manor Recreation Center on the second Wednesday from August through December. Speakers are featured at the meetings.

Writers 4 Kids

Mark Newhouse
Writers Group Leader

The Writers 4 Kids (Sumter County) meets at the Hibiscus Recreation Center on Fridays every month. Helping writers who want to write for children, pre-K to young adult, is focus of the meetings. Mark Newhouse is the Group Leader

Port Orange Scribes

Ben Collins and Peggy Lambert
Writers Group Leaders

The Port Orange Scribes (Volusia County) meets at the Grace Episcopal Church on the first and third Wednesdays every month. Speakers, critiques, discussions, and readings are featured at the meetings. Ben Collins and Peggy Lambert are the Group Leaders.

Villa Writers

Melody Dimick
Writers Group Leader

The Villa Writers (Volusia County) meets on the second and fourth Thursdays every month. Speakers, critiques, discussions, and readings are featured at the meetings. Melody Dimick is the Group Leader.

Out of State Writers Groups

Reno Writing Clinic

Eugene and Dodie Orlando
Writers Group Leaders

The Reno Writing Clinic (out-of-state) meets at the Aroma Club Café on Monday every month. Critiques, discussions, and readings are featured at the meetings. Eugene and Dodie Orlando are the Group Leaders.

Index of Contributors

www.ingramcontent.com/pod-product-compliance
Lightning Source LLC
Chambersburg PA
CBHW022012090426
42741CB00007B/997